At David C Cook, we equip the local church around
the corner and around the globe to make disciples.
Come see how we are working together—go to
www.davidccook.com. Thank you!

transforming lives together

What people are saying about …

THE FRESH EYES SERIES

"I heard Doug speak over a decade ago on the feeding of the five thousand, and I still remember what he said. He brought the familiar story to life in a way that made me see it all unfold. I remember thinking, *What would I have done if I'd been there that day with Jesus?* That's why Doug's writing is so valuable. God recorded these events in His Word and Doug takes readers to those moments in history and makes them relatable and best of all, memorable."

—Robin Jones Gunn, bestselling author
of over ninety books including the Christy
Miller series and *Victim of Grace*

"On a visit to Japan, our translator asked an artist working in gold leaf how it felt to be surrounded by such expensive materials. The artist replied, 'I've been working with gold so long, I've forgotten it's value.' I know I've felt that exact way when it comes to reading the Word of God. I've been working/reading/studying it for so long, I'm ashamed to say that sometimes, even though I love God's Word, I've forgotten it's value. That's why I'm so grateful for Fresh Eyes. Doug has taken the familiar stories of Scripture, and given us new ideas to ponder, angles to look from, and context to understand. A reminder of the richness and value that surrounds us every day."

—**Kathi Lipp**, bestselling author of *The Husband Project*, *Clutter Free*, and *Overwhelmed*

"The Fresh Eyes series is nothing less than amazing—the most profound, to the point, original, awe-inspiring, and challenging writings about Jesus and the Bible I have ever read or imagined! I was immediately stunned by how the subject matter is exactly what I've always been looking for in Scripture! I hope there will be millions of Christians like me who learn to see Scripture with fresh eyes."

—**Jorge Casas**, bassist, Grammy-award winning producer

"These books are a hit. Doug has found a profound and compelling way to have the reader (ordinary people like you and me) have the eyes of our hearts enlightened. I have read the entire Bible, front to back, for the past fourteen years. In these books, I have gained new insight into Bible sayings, Jesus' miracles, and Jesus' parables. I gained fresh insight into what God is saying to me. In my 162 MLB game schedule, each day brings new excitement. Doug's writing and dissecting of verses make each verse exciting as I grew deeper in my relationship with our Lord."

—**David Jauss**, Major League baseball coach, Pittsburgh Pirates

"Jesus spoke of unique teachers who were able to bring 'new treasures' out of their storerooms (Matt. 13:52). Doug Newton is an extraordinary author who brings us 'new treasure' in this Fresh Eyes series. This series imparts the rare gift of seeing Scripture with fresh eyes, thus igniting fresh fire in our lives for Jesus and His mission. I highly recommend this series for anyone desiring a personal revival and an expanded faith for how greatly God can use their lives. I experienced this for myself as I read Doug's life-giving words!"

—**Larry Walkemeyer**, D.Min.; pastor; church planter; Director of Equipping—Exponential; author of *15 Characteristics of Effective Pastors*

"Doug Newton is a skilled and passionate communicator as well as a trusted, wise guide both from the pulpit and the printed page. His Fresh Eyes series draws from clear thought, engaged storytelling, and a worthy message to help readers marvel anew over God's love and sustain their faith in the face of today's challenges."

—**Ivan L. Filby**, PhD, president of Greenville University, IL

"For many who cherish the Bible as God's Word, a daily experience with the Bible has no greater impact than a weather report, an Op-Ed piece, or a blog post. This is because few believers actually read the Bible much and, when they do, they give it only superficial attention. In the Fresh Eyes series, Doug Newton demonstrates how familiar miracle stories, well-known parables, and often-cited gospel sayings can come alive with power to expose small and limited horizons and expand them to wider and deeper perceptions of kingdom reality then draw you in as Newton teases out life-changing biblical implications."

—**Bishop David W. Kendall**, PhD, Free Methodist Church—USA

"For decades Doug Newton's clear and crisp teaching has captured the deep and transformative truths of God's Word. What a treasure to have these rich and wonderful insights through Fresh Eyes. You will be deeply touched and truly challenged by this brilliant master teacher. What a gift!"

—**David Goodnight**, JD, LLM,
partner at Stoel Rives, LLP

"Doug Newton reminds us that the compelling teachings and miracles of Jesus were not just clever events to create believers but were the examples of everyday life. In captivating stories, Newton refocuses us to remember that staying 'tuned in' in prayerful communion opens our eyes to the reality that miracles happen all around us all the time."

—**Hal Conklin**, president of USA
Green Communities, former mayor
of Santa Barbara, California

"Fresh Eyes is a crucial series for our hyper-connected world. Doug Newton equips readers with the tools needed to slow down, open our eyes, and unlock the true meaning of the inspired stories of the Bible. As he has done from the pulpit for many years, Doug provides rich guidance and training with easy-to-understand language and stories that make things click. Fresh Eyes is a must-have for anyone who wants to be equipped to wrestle with the meaning of Scripture and the many ways it applies to the hustle and bustle of twenty-first-century living.

—**Hugo Perez**, chief marketing
officer, OHorizons Foundation

DOUG NEWTON

FRESH

EYES

ON

JESUS'

MIRACLES

Discovering New Insights in Familiar Passages

DAVID C COOK

transforming lives together

FRESH EYES ON JESUS' MIRACLES
Published by David C Cook
4050 Lee Vance Drive
Colorado Springs, CO 80918 U.S.A.

Integrity Music Limited, a Division of David C Cook
Eastbourne, East Sussex BN23 6NT, England

The graphic circle C logo is a registered trademark of David C Cook.

LCCN 2017964687
ISBN 978-1-4347-1211-0
eISBN 978-1-4347-1214-1

© 2018 Douglas M. Newton
Published in association with the literary agency of Books & Such
Literary Management, 52 Mission Circle, Suite 122, PMB 170,
Santa Rosa, CA 95409-5370, www.booksandsuch.com.

The Team: Alice Crider, Mick Silva, Amy Konyndyk,
Rachael Stevenson, Diane Gardner, Susan Murdock
Cover Design: Nick Lee

Printed in the United States of America
First Edition 2018

1 2 3 4 5 6 7 8 9 10

051618

*In memory of William L. Lane, whose scholarship,
friendship, and encouragement convinced me
that the biblical record of miracles is credible
and the expectation of ongoing miracles is
reasonable and central for followers of Jesus.*

CONTENTS

ACKNOWLEDGMENTS

The man who was, I think, the most creative and engaging preacher I ever heard died in a car crash when I was in sixth grade. I say "I think" because I never really cared about what he was saying at the time. After all, I was only twelve years old, and there were better things to do to pass the time until noon. But I sensed his impact because of the way my parents and all the other adults in my small country church reacted when he preached. They loved it—and him. The congregation leaned forward. Even our 1965 Chevy Impala seemed eager for church every Sunday!

Carl Johnson, our pastor, a journalism grad student at Syracuse University, apparently mixed humor with ways to enter a biblical text that disposed of the traditional three-point sermon with the tearjerker story at the end. Again I say "apparently" because I didn't get the jokes or insights; I just heard the appreciative laughs and appreciable amens around me.

And even though I vowed at age ten I would never be a preacher, I knew what a preacher needed to be from sitting in the pews Sunday after Sunday inside that atmosphere of rapt attention. So when I did eventually become a pastor-teacher—even though my "call" was initially more coincidental than covenantal—I had an unchosen but unwavering passion: to help people see the Bible with fresh eyes and expectancy.

Now that forty years of preaching and teaching have passed, I can see how the "spirit" of Carl Johnson—I should really capitalize that word—permeated and still permeates how I approach biblical examination and exposition. That Spirit led me to preach two back-to-back sermons one Sunday while running the entire time on a treadmill in order to illustrate the significance of Peter's use of the word *spoudazo* (meaning "make every effort") in 2 Peter 1:5. It led me to build and preach inside a black cloth-covered enclosure just so I could come to the finale and demonstrate with one thrust of a spear how praise and proclamation pierce spiritual darkness.

I never wanted to use gimmicks, but very often the Lord prompted me to see something unusual and use something visual. As a result, I have enjoyed kind comments from the people of four congregations over the years telling me how much they looked forward to what I was going to do and say on Sunday. I always deflected those comments with "You mean, what the *Lord* is going to say." And they would nod, "Of course."

However, the fact remains that the human role of careful study and creativity combine to make what God wants to say through His Word clear and compelling. Creativity is inherently mnemonic.

At the outset of this Fresh Eyes series, I want to acknowledge Carl Johnson and the gifted thinkers and teachers he represents who have inspired me toward preaching that reveals rather than regurgitates truth. And even more, I thank all the congregations of believers among whom I have lived and served who have shown me what it looks like to lean forward to hear a word from the Lord: for three years with the kids of the South Presbyterian Church high school group in Syracuse, New York; for thirteen years with the people of Fountain Square Church in Bowling Green, Kentucky; for five years with the students and staff of the Oakdale Christian Academy boarding school in Jackson, Kentucky; and for the past eleven years with the people of Greenville (IL) Free Methodist Church.

For fifteen years I served as editor of *Light & Life*, the denominational magazine of the Free Methodist Church. This was also a significant time in my life when I learned to communicate more broadly through writing to people I would never see from the Sunday pulpit. That opportunity and training would never have occurred without the courage of four bishops who hired me—a pastor with no journalism or seminary degree—simply because I had what they regarded as an anointed, albeit "unsafe" (their word), creative approach to communication.

My role as editor led to my speaking periodically at writer's conferences—most often at the renowned Mount Hermon Christian Writers Conference. I owe a great debt of thanks to Dave Talbott, who hardly knew me when inviting me to preach on Palm Sunday in 1998 in the rustic auditorium beneath the praising redwoods to the crowd filled with professional writers. And he continued to do so for several years, even though I had not yet joined the ranks of published authors.

That is where I was first heard and shaped by these professionals, many of whom became friends. One of them, Wendy Lawton, committed herself to me as my agent long before there was any sign I would ever repay her kindness with even a dime of compensation. I couldn't have been given a more gifted, wise, and dedicated agent than she and the Books & Such Literary Agency.

One day she and Janet Grant, founder of the agency, approached me with a clear vision of how to position me as an author. They said, "You need to just do what you do—open people's eyes to Scripture in fresh ways." Within a few months, I had a contract with David C Cook thanks to them and Alice Crider, senior acquisitions editor, who championed this multi-book project with an accompanying app.

Suddenly I had a contract, and the initial draft of three books had to be written from scratch in five months. This was a daunting task made more feasible, because over the years I have learned how to write with intense focus as my Greenville church staff graciously accommodated my need to get away several times a year to work on various writing projects.

However, when this massive project came along I needed something more than intense focus. I would need big blocks of time and a sense of the Lord's permission. A series of God-ordained events gave me that green light and changed my ministry responsibilities dramatically. Two of those events involved divine instruction that came miraculously and separately through Ben Dodson and Sarah Vanderkwaak. I am grateful they risked speaking when they could have remained silent. I am also grateful for dear friends Ivan and Kathie Filby, and my gifted superintendent Ben Tolly, for seeing a future ahead of me I would not have imagined.

Alice Crider was gracious enough to honor my request to select my own editor, Mick Silva. We had met at Mount Hermon and had only two casual conversations, but that was enough for me to have confidence in his spiritual sensitivity and professional skills. This initial confidence proved to be well-founded as our friendship grew and as Mick's expertise sharpened and supported the mission and message of the Fresh Eyes books chapter by chapter and line by line.

I was also pleased to have been brought into the David C Cook family at a time when the company was retooling its focus and functions in fresh ways to fulfill its longstanding mission to resource and disciple the church worldwide. That mission, so evident in the processes and people at David C Cook, convinced my wife and me to come under their banner in this project. I have enjoyed how much I have learned every step of the way through the enthusiastic encouragement of Alice Crider, Toben Heim, and the team of people assigned to guide me through this project to completion and distribution: Rachael Stevenson, Diane Gardner,

Kayla Fenstermaker, Amy Konyndyk, Nick Lee, Susan Murdock, Megan Stengel, Annette Brickbealer, Nathan Landry, and Austin Davco.

Finally, it probably goes without saying, but it is impossible not to shout from the rooftops how much I owe to my family. My two girls, their amazing husbands, and combined five kids. They have not only given me their love and respect over the years, but also what it means to live life knowing your kids are proud of you—and tell you! That lubricates the mechanics of life through the grind of large projects like Fresh Eyes.

Then there's Margie. She's my hero, my model, my friend, my encourager. There has been a sparkle in her eyes from the very beginning of being "us" that comes from her love for Jesus. That sparkle is my north star. It keeps me navigating through life, no matter what comes, toward greater love for the Lord. Without that sparkle in her eyes, my own would have long since grown dim with cares and worries and doubts preventing me from seeing anything—life itself and its Author—with fresh eyes. But when you have someone who loves you unconditionally in such a way that helps you know the love of God, your eyes will sparkle too with expectancy for seeing new and fresh things in the world and in the Word.

Doug Newton
March 2018

ABOUT THE FRESH EYES SERIES

What if the commonplace understanding of a Bible story or a well-known Scripture passage is the very thing keeping us from seeing the text in a new, life-transforming way?

We all find ourselves facing this problem when we study the Bible. We believe Scripture is living and powerful. But many of us, after a genuine encounter with God followed by faithful Bible study and many sermons, became so familiar with Scripture that it lost its impact. The Bible became a book of riddles to be solved. Once we "figured out what a passage meant," we checked it off and moved on. We've seen these stories too many times, and everyone who's been a Christian for even a year or two knows how that voracious appetite for the Word quickly fades.

Pastors and Bible teachers craft a message from a particular text, and the lesson they convey becomes the way we understand the passage from that point on. Within a few short years, it feels like we're hearing the same thing over and over again. We begin to approach the Bible with less zip and zeal. Familiarity may not always breed contempt, but it does tend to breed complacency.

Yet consider Jesus' remedy: "You have heard that it was said, but I tell you …" He invited His listeners to break away from well-worn thinking to see something new, different. We need to look with fresh eyes at what we think we know well. A passage's common interpretation may have taken a wrong turn somewhere along the line and been passed along like an urban legend. The application may need to shift in a different direction or include something not considered before. There's new hope for our lives to change when we can say, "I never saw it that way before."

My primary mission with this book series is not to share new insights I've uncovered. My greater desire is to reveal specific techniques that will allow you to make new discoveries about familiar passages that can revive your love for the infinite Word and transform your work in teaching and testimony.

The interactive section at the end of each chapter includes a "Vision Check," which describes Fresh Eyes study techniques. These reveal how I found something new and inspiring by reexamining the text and context of a passage, the life situations involved, the cultural perspectives reflected, and other details and how I began to see Scripture more imaginatively. You'll also find more resources on dougnewton.com and the Fresh Eyes app to help you gain additional insights.

I pray you find that the treasures in God's Word are truly inexhaustible when you come with fresh eyes.

INTRODUCTION

Many of my good friends over the years have been Bible scholars. That's how I know I am not one myself. I need help translating Greek, and I can't read Hebrew at all. I know little about what is called the "intertestamental period" and can't remember the difference between Hermann Gunkel and Herman Munster.

But I've been a pastor for forty years and have seen what the words of Scripture can do in the hearts and lives of people who can't even read at all, much less read in an archaic language. The power of God's Word astounds. I've witnessed a young man come to faith, though he smoked marijuana nightly, because he was reading a copy of the Psalms he found left behind on a restaurant table. The words, though he could barely comprehend them, were so powerful that he ditched the joints and embraced the high he experienced with God. I've seen a thirty-something woman liberated from a prison of past satanic rituals and sacrifices after she was simply asked to read a divinely selected psalm aloud. And I've watched countless people facing grief, fear, shame, or confusion find sudden soothing peace and strengthening hope from nothing more than a verse or two. Perhaps you could share a similar experience.

None of these people needed to know anything about the questions biblical scholars grapple with. Probably none were aware that the most reliable early manuscripts do not include the story of the woman caught in adultery in John 8, yet they could find ecstatic emancipation in Jesus' words, "Neither do I condemn you" (v. 11), as if He had spoken those words to them personally.

Interaction with God through His Word is a miraculous affair, especially when we approach it as if for the first time. So we should search the familiar miracle stories for new insights.

The discoveries found in the ten miracles we'll explore are presented in an order that parallels what must be any disciple's journey toward spiritual maturity and fruitfulness:

- What kingdom values (as opposed to worldly attitudes and norms) does the miracle reveal?

- With those truths in mind, how should our beliefs change?

- How then should our actions change?

These steps can (and do) happen concurrently when we study God's Word, as we trust Him more fully, follow Him more closely, and fulfill His purposes by His grace and power. But it all begins with a God-given "Spirit of wisdom and revelation" that "the eyes of your heart may be enlightened" (Eph. 1:17–18). That's always the ongoing miracle.

GOT WINE?

Turning Water into Wine

John 2:1–11

If God is able to turn water into wine, why
don't we see more cases of transformation
in people and circumstances?

I pastored for years in southern Kentucky, where the humid summers make you sweat like a cold glass of sweet iced tea. This was usually not a problem, provided you could go from your air-conditioned home to your air-conditioned car to your air-conditioned workplace to the air-conditioned store.

But on too many occasions I had the misfortune of performing weddings in non-air-conditioned churches chosen for their quaint ambience. Funny how the allure of ambience wilts as the congregation waits for the bride's entry. Every bride wants a perfect wedding day. Did no one think the lack of air conditioning might be a distracting discomfort? Oh well …

Some things are the same in all places at all times. Weddings need to go well. That's why even two thousand years later we can relate to the first miracle the apostle John recorded in his gospel. It occurred during a wedding in Cana. The problem at this wedding was not drenching humidity but the disappointing lack of celebratory wine.

Before we delve into the miracle and discover something you may never have thought about, it's important to realize that this miracle holds a special place in the New Testament Gospels. Only John's gospel tells it. Matthew, Mark, and Luke for some reason did not include it. On top of that, John handpicked just seven miracles out of scores he could have chosen. He did so because his mission differed from the other gospel writers'. The few miracles he chose ranked at the top of all Jesus' miracles, because in John's mind they were not just supernatural wonders. They were "miraculous signs" pointing to Jesus' divine identity and unique mission.

John chose this miraculous sign to be the first—the leadoff hitter for his whole story of Jesus' glory. We can only guess why. But what could be a better start to the gospel of Jesus than to show Him to be the one who can do miracles of transformation? Isn't that what everyone needs?

John started by saying, "On the third day a wedding took place at Cana in Galilee. Jesus' mother was there, and Jesus and his disciples had also been invited to the wedding. When the wine was gone, Jesus' mother said to him, 'They have no more wine'" (John 2:1–3).

Notice those last five words Jesus' mother spoke. Don't just read them. Imagine them. What did she sound like when she voiced them? Certainly she wasn't flat and emotionless like a computer speech synthesizer: "They … have … no … more … wine."

Imagine her tone of voice. Her volume. Her intensity. A little cultural background might help inform your imagination.

In those days, wedding celebrations were major events that often lasted several days. You think wedding planners today have a chore? Imagine having the job of "master of the banquet." Some translations even call that person the "governor of the feast" (KJV). A wedding celebration was no small affair if it required a governor to be in charge!

With so much riding on a wedding celebration attended by the whole town, you can imagine the potential outcry if things went poorly. In fact, according to historians, running out of wine at a wedding celebration was grounds for a lawsuit! And you thought we live in a litigious society?

That's why worry and a shot of desperation probably resonated in Jesus' mother's voice. Perhaps she pulled Jesus aside and whispered it, but there would have been a lot of force behind those words, like a pressure valve releasing pent-up steam: "They have no more wine!"

If you, like me, grew up in a teetotaler home, running out of wine would cause great relief not grave consternation. So I wonder what would give me a similar level of concern, considering my upbringing. Here's the best I can do: What if they ran out of wedding cake, the kind I love piled high with frosting? I imagine myself attending a wedding in the humid Kentucky heat … and trapped in a church basement after the ceremony, waiting uncomfortably, dress shirt sticking to the back of the chair … longing for—no, praying for—the good fortune of getting a corner piece of cake adorned with a creamy confection rose. Then finally getting to the buffet table and finding they've run out of cake! Yes, I would be considering a lawsuit! Or maybe something even worse involving that cake knife!

Somehow that imagined scenario puts me in a place where I can hear Mary's panic when she cries, "They have no more wine." Yet despite her desperation, Jesus seemed unmoved. Let's read on: "'Woman, why do you involve me?' Jesus replied. 'My hour has not yet come'" (John 2:4).

How would you like to get a Mother's Day card addressed "Woman"? Maybe that was a respectful form of address in Jesus' day, but He still sounds reluctant to help. Is He really being unsympathetic? Probably not. He was making a theological point. When He referred to "my hour," He was not talking about clock time. The word used here refers to a "special moment." He typically referred to His eventual death on the cross this way.

Jesus was putting things in proper perspective. He knew His mother wanted Him to use His supernatural ability to fix the problem, which He knew would reveal something about His amazing identity. But was it time for that? Shouldn't He reserve that revelation for a greater display of glory than solving this wine shortage? I can almost hear Him say, "I came into this world to save much more than one wedding." That's where He was probably coming from when He replied to His mother.

Amusingly, Jesus' mother didn't seem to wait for His reply before she was off rounding up the servants. After all, she was His mother. She knew her boy. She didn't need to wait for an answer before assuming He would help. John recorded, "His mother said to the servants, 'Do whatever he tells you.' Nearby stood six stone water jars, the kind used by the Jews for ceremonial washing, each holding from twenty to thirty gallons" (vv. 5–6).

Remember that fact given about the stone water jars. We'll come back to them.

Jesus ordered the servants to fill the jars with water and then take a sample of the water to the master of the banquet. When they did that, the feast master, not knowing the whole story, enjoyed what he considered a fine glass of wine. But that puzzled him: "Then he called the bridegroom aside and said, 'Everyone brings out the choice wine first and then the cheaper wine after the guests have had too much to drink; but you have saved the best till now'" (vv. 9–10).

Not only did Jesus convert water into wine, but it was not the boxed variety! This wine would impress the snootiest waiter at restaurants where common people can't even afford to pay for parking.

Think about that. Jesus took water, which consists of only two elements: two parts hydrogen, one part oxygen (H_2O). Not only did He remix those two elements, but He also added the element carbon. We know that because the natural sugars in wine grapes include carbon. And He introduced many more compounds that never existed in the water. Wine includes tannins and organic acids: tartaric, malic, and citric. In short, He didn't just sneak some red food coloring into the water when no one was looking. He somehow accelerated the aging process and turned two minutes into years, as far as the wine was concerned.

Without even waving His hand or whispering "Abracadabra," Jesus performed a miracle of radical transformation. Only the God who created the universe from nothing could have infused the one-time water with carbon and acids and sparkling flavor. If He could do this to water-filled pots, imagine what He can do with worry-filled people. Imagine how He can create unexpectedly high-quality wisdom or faith or peace where none exists.

Isn't this the basis of our hope, our only hope—that God performs miracles of transformation? So let's return to the teaser question at the head of this chapter: If God is able to turn water into wine, why don't we see more cases of transformation in people and circumstances?

The answer emerges when we backtrack to the command Jesus gave the servants and note their response. Remember, Jesus told them to fill the waterpots. Picture those waterpots. Recall that each one held twenty to thirty gallons of water, so they were about the size of a standard galvanized trashcan, except made of stone.

How would the servants have fulfilled Jesus' command? Would they have pulled out the garden hose, attached it to a house spigot, and lopped it over the top? Probably not.

Would they have carried the waterpots to the town well, filled them, and lugged them back to the festivities? Thirty gallons of water weighs about 250 pounds, and that's on top of the weight of the stone waterpots themselves. No way would even two people be able to carry such a heavy, sloshing, unwieldy container. Even a donkey cart would have proved pointless no matter how hard you tried to keep the pots steady and level over the rough paths.

So how would they have filled the waterpots? By carrying small buckets back and forth from the well, probably located some distance away, over and over again until the pots were full.

I'm a pretty hard worker, but the idea of hauling water back and forth in little two-gallon animal skin buckets would not have been a pleasant thought. Bear in mind I probably had already filled those waterpots earlier in the day.

What would I have done? What would you have done? We should not zip right past this question in order to get on with the miracle story. I got out my calculator and estimated it would have taken about eighty trips back and forth to obey Jesus' command. Or perhaps only forty trips if using a neck yoke for carrying two skins at a time. Either way, the task was time consuming and labor intensive.

If I had been a servant in this story, I might have filled the first waterpot to within a couple inches of the top, thought *That's good enough*, and started filling waterpot number two. I would have filled that one to within perhaps three or four inches of the top, thought again *That's good enough*, and started in on waterpot number three. I would have filled pot three to within five or six inches…. You see where I'm going? My enthusiasm to fulfill Jesus' command would have been draining out even as I was filling the waterpots, until maybe—maybe—the sixth and final waterpot would have been about half-full when I decided to draw one more bucket and a final conclusion: *That's good enough.*

However, here's the shocking observation about the text. John carefully pointed out that the servants "filled them to the brim" (John 2:7). Most servants in this culture could choose how they went about their work, like employees in our day. That's why in several places the New Testament urges Christian servants to work diligently and with good attitudes as an act of worship and witness. I must confess the servants at the wedding were more thorough and diligent than I would have been. But what difference does it make whether they filled the waterpots to the maximum level?

Here's the difference. Imagine my sixth half-full waterpot containing only fifteen gallons of water compared with the actual servants' completely full waterpot. How much wine would I have gotten? Fifteen gallons. How many gallons of wine would they have gotten? Thirty. If I had brought five gallons of water, how much wine would I have gotten? Five gallons. Do you see the point?

Yes, Jesus could have turned a thimble of water into thirty gallons of wine. But John reported a miracle not of multiplication but of transformation. Jesus intentionally "revealed his glory" (v. 11) by changing the quality not the quantity of the substance brought to Him. He could have snapped His fingers and created enough wine for a thousand weddings, but He chose to remedy the wine shortage by telling the servants to bring to Him what needed to be changed.

Only Jesus could have performed the miracle of transformation. He took H_2O and made an elegant combination of elements, tannin, bouquet, and color—from water to fine wine—without touching, adding, mixing, or blending any additional ingredients. But the amount of water that was transformed depended on how much water the servants brought. Had they brought less water, less would have been transformed.

That's the lesson for us. It turns out that the old gospel song has been right all along:

> What a Friend we have in Jesus,
> All our sins and griefs to bear!
> What a privilege to carry
> Everything to God in prayer!
> O what peace we often forfeit,
> O what needless pain we bear,
> All because we do not carry
> Everything to God in prayer.[1]

Why don't we see more transformation in people and circumstances? The amount of wine we enjoy depends on the amount of water—things that need to be changed—we bring to Jesus, particularly when brought in the waterpots of prayer. How many gallons are you bringing?

Documentation and analyses of spiritual revivals throughout history reveal that prior to these events, people "filled [the waterpots] to the brim" with prayer. What is true of widespread revivals is true of restored marriages, rescued addicts, redeemed prodigals, and rejuvenated hope: prayer should be thorough to the point of nearly overflowing. Whatever needs to be transformed, take it to Jesus in prayer. And do not stop until you experience an incredible transformation either in your world or in how you see it.

It will be like getting the corner piece of a wedding cake over and over again.

20/20 FOCUS

1. In Scripture, miracles often include some human involvement. Can you think of other biblical examples when human involvement contributed to the occurrence or impact of a miracle? What does that reveal about God's purposes? Why do you think He'd want us contributing to His miracles?

2. What more do you need to bring to Jesus to be transformed in prayer?

3. Have you ever truly considered how much forfeited peace and needless pain we suffer from not bringing "everything to God in prayer"? Why do you think you have had a hard time filling the waterpots with prayer?

4. Is there something else you saw in this story that changes the way you understand it?

Lord, I thank You that You alone can utterly transform any resource, any situation, or any person into something brand new, exciting, and more fitting to Your purpose. Forgive my lack of trust and when I withhold things, try to fix my problems, and attempt change myself or my situations without looking to You first. Help me fill my life up with prayer to the brim. Amen.

VISION CHECK

The study technique this chapter employed involves more fully imagining yourself in the story. Ask, *What would I have been experiencing in this situation?*

Read Genesis 12, which tells of God's promise to Abram to make him the father of a great nation. Put yourself in Abram's situation as an elderly man with a barren wife. What might you have been thinking had you been in his place? Write down what insights come to mind and, using dougnewton.com or the Fresh Eyes app, compare them with a few that came to my mind.

2

TIME WILL TELL

Healing the Royal Official's Son
John 4:46–54

Sometimes you have to forget what
you've always heard in order to
see what you've never seen.

I once heard a renowned astrophysicist boast on a morning news program that he and other colleagues can now describe what happened at the beginning of the universe to within the first few billionths of a second. He admitted those first couple of billionths were still a mystery. However, perhaps expecting pushback from committed theists in the audience, he quickly asked people not to get him wrong. He was not saying there is no God; he was just saying that with respect to the origin of the universe, there was nothing for a god to do.

In other words, from his point of view, astrophysics did not automatically contradict the first few words of the Bible: "In the beginning God …" (Gen. 1:1). For all science knows, a Supreme Being might have been present in the beginning, but He was merely an arms-folded bystander. I won't even begin to bombard this scientist's claim with the host of classic philosophical arguments for God's existence as Creator. I simply ask you to consider that immeasurably brief moment just before the beginning when there was nothing and then there was something.

Is it really possible for something—energy or matter—to come out of nothing without the causal action of a nonmaterial entity? In another context, in his poem "The Hollow Men," T. S. Eliot wrote about an inscrutable shadow between the possibility of something existing and it actually occurring.

> Between the idea
> And the reality
>
> . . . .
>
> Between the conception
> And the creation
>
> . . . .
>
> Between the desire
> And the spasm
> Between the potency
> And the existence
>
> . . . .
>
> Falls the Shadow[1]

People who trust Scripture's testimony believe God's Word sheds light on that shadowed moment just as the universe began. Whatever you may believe about the timing of creation events, Holy Scripture declares one paramount fact: the only true God created everything by the power of His word.

Keep this in mind as we focus on the miracle of Jesus healing the royal official's dying son. But first, to see this text with fresh eyes, you must paradoxically and intentionally put yourself in the dark. Sometimes in order to see what you've never seen before, you have to forget whatever you've heard before.

Think of it this way. When you watch a movie with a surprise ending the second time, you can no longer be surprised. You probably won't watch with rapt attention as you did the first time. You might even go get a snack while the movie still plays, because you know you won't miss anything. In the same way, we tend to read familiar Scripture passages with less than rapt attention. So the secret to approaching this and many other familiar passages is to pretend you've never read it before and you don't know how it turns out. That's hard to do, but as you will see in this case, everything hangs on *not* knowing what you already know.

This miracle began with a royal official whose son was dying in Capernaum, a town about eighteen miles from where Jesus was staying in Cana. In a last-ditch attempt to save his son's life, the royal official sought out Jesus to ask Him to go back with him and heal his son. That's as far as we should go now or else we will start dragging in ideas we need to forget. You'll see what I mean later.

DETECTIVE WORK: THE ETD AND ETA

Our task is to reconstruct this miracle's timeline the way detectives try to solve a crime. So let's hunt for time references in the story. Here's what we find: "When he [the royal official] inquired as to the time when his son got better, they said to him, 'Yesterday, at one in the afternoon'" (John 4:52).

Notice there are two key reference points. The word *yesterday* tells us the story spans two days. Each day involves one key event. The first day—let's call it Monday—is the day the royal official found Jesus and asked Him to come heal his son. That happened at what Jews of that day would have called the "seventh hour," which is equivalent to our 1:00 p.m. At that moment, Jesus said to the man, "Go,… your son will live" (v. 50). Then sometime on the second day (Tuesday) "while he was still on the way, his servants met him with the news that his boy was living" (v. 51).

Simple enough. However, the timeline reveals more we need to reconstruct, things not explicitly spelled out in the text. If we make a couple reasonable assumptions consistent with the facts of the story, you'll be surprised at what we discover.

We need to ask the following two questions: When did the man leave home to go find Jesus? And when did the man head back home after meeting with Jesus? The first question is the most important to our fresh insight. When did the man leave home?

Let's assume he felt a sense of urgency and left home early in the morning on Monday, the same day he found Jesus. Why? Could be to protect himself from the dishonor of losing a male descendant. Yet this is the second of only seven miracles John reported, and he elevated love throughout his gospel. So maybe John was moved by this desperate love for a son, a man not wanting to leave his child's bedside any longer than necessary.

I remember the day my mother died. She was in hospice. All the signs pointed to death within just a few hours. So my wife and I simply waited by her bedside. She was not conscious and most likely never would regain consciousness. Nevertheless, there was no way either of us was going to leave her bedside. It's a very human desire to be present in those last moments. And what if she did rouse and we weren't there for her?

Now transport that fact into this story, along with the more compelling reality that the key persons are a young boy and a father who would do anything to save his son. For the father, the idea of leaving his son's side, of *not* being there in case he roused for a few minutes, would have been unthinkable. Unless … there was a slight possibility … a last hope?

Put yourself in the father's place. He heard that Jesus—who many people assumed was some kind of prophet with healing powers—was in Cana. What are you going to do? You're going to leave your suffering son, conscious or unconscious, and make the trip as quickly as you can to try to bring help. But you would do everything in your power to return as quickly as you could. That's what the father must have had in mind. So when did he leave for Cana to find Jesus? It's reasonable to assume he did not leave until Monday morning. The facts located in both the text and in the geography of the area support that theory.

Capernaum, where the boy lay dying, was eighteen miles from Cana, where Jesus was. Walking at a steady pace, the father could be in Cana in about six hours. Admittedly, we who live in an automobile culture might find the prospect of walking eighteen miles daunting. But the father's culture was pedestrian. People were used to walking. True, eighteen miles is still eighteen miles. But hey, who cared? His son was dying!

If we assume he left Monday morning, a six-hour trip would put him in Cana—you guessed it—right around the "seventh hour" (adding a little time for him to locate Jesus once he got into town). Fits the text, doesn't it?

DETECTIVE WORK: A HIDDEN DELAY

Now let's add to the timeline, and you'll see something puzzling. The man and Jesus had a brief conversation that couldn't have taken more than two or three minutes. Here's what Scripture records: "When this man heard that Jesus had arrived in Galilee from Judea, he went to him and begged him to come and heal his son, who was close to death. 'Unless you people see signs and wonders,' Jesus told him, 'you will never believe.' The royal official said, 'Sir, come down before my child dies.' 'Go,' Jesus replied, 'your son will live'" (John 4:47–50).

After that brief exchange it was probably about 1:05 p.m. What did the man do next? Remarkably, the text says, "The man took Jesus at his word and departed" (v. 50).

At this point the text rushes us right along, and we tend not to pause and put two and two together. The next verse says, "While he was still on the way ..." (v. 51). If we read too quickly, we picture the man leaving Jesus and immediately heading home. But that's not what he did. How do we know? Because he didn't meet his servants on the road until the next day. This is incredible! He did not rush right home. He could have made it. It was only 1:05. Yes, he had already walked eighteen miles that day, and another eighteen would have been a challenge. But again, who cared? His son was dying!

If I were in that situation I would glance at my watch, calculate when I could get home, realize I could be there before nightfall, take into consideration that it would be an easier and quicker trip being a downward slope from Cana to Capernaum, and would have hightailed it. Within a mile of home, I would have quickened my pace even more, probably breaking out into a sprint when I neared my street and saw my house in the distance. Then I would have burst through the front door, breathlessly shouting, "Is he alive? Is he alive?"

Yet a loving father who went to desperate lengths to seek Jesus' help on the chance He would drop everything and come heal his boy didn't head home on Monday. He waited around

Cana until Tuesday morning with no email or phone to check on his son. His hope rested in Jesus' word, and he took it to heart. That's remarkable faith! I'd love to have that kind of confidence in Jesus' reassuring words. But hold your horses; you know too much. It's not the kind of faith we think it is. Let's move on.

DETECTIVE WORK: DELAYED BELIEF

There's one more crucial observation. Notice the father's reaction when he met the servants on his way home: "While he was still on the way, his servants met him with the news that his boy was living. When he inquired as to the time when his son got better, they said to him, 'Yesterday, at one in the afternoon, the fever left him.' Then the father realized that this was the exact time at which Jesus had said to him, 'Your son will live.' So he and his whole household believed" (John 4:51–53).

John, our gospel writer, was very clear that the man did not actually "believe" in Jesus until *after* receiving word about his son's recovery. Wait a minute! If he didn't even believe until then, what was going on when he "took Jesus at his word and departed" (v. 50)?

Now is the time to forget what we already know about what happened. We know (because we've seen the movie) that *Jesus healed the boy long-distance.* The royal official did not know that. Jesus did *not* say, "You may go; I will heal your son long-distance." All Jesus said was, "Your son will live" (v. 50).

How would the royal official have understood what Jesus meant? In the same way you understand a doctor who comes into the waiting room after performing critical surgery on your loved one. He walks in, you put down your magazine and lean in for his report, and he says, "You can all rest easy. The surgery went fine. Your dad is doing well. You can see him in a couple of hours."

In that moment, you are not hearing him claim to have performed a miracle. You're hearing a report from someone who you believe has the necessary experience and knowledge to give you accurate and authoritative information. He knows what he's talking about. That's what puts you at ease. You take his word and depart for some supper in the hospital cafeteria.

That explains the father's reaction to Jesus' words. Jesus, widely hailed as a prophet-healer, informed the royal official that his son would live. The father was hearing a prediction from someone who he believed had the authority to give accurate information about the future.

"Wow! I thought for sure my son was going to die. Everything pointed in that direction, but Jesus said he will live. That's great news! I can relax. I'll wait till morning to head home."

But then on his way, somewhere along the dusty road from Cana to Capernaum, he saw through the shimmering heat the wavy images of figures coming toward him. He was genuinely surprised when he drew close enough to recognize his own servants coming his way. I imagine this conversation:

"What are you guys doing here?"

"We had to bring you the news about your son."

"What news? Is he still alive? Did he die? What?"

"He's alive and all better."

"All better? Jesus said he would live, but he's better already? I thought it would still take a while, considering how sick he was."

"No. He's totally better! Up and eating. Normal."

"Wow! When did that happen?"

"Oh, about one o'clock yesterday."

"Yesterday? About one?" He drops his head and pauses to calculate, when it dawns on him. "I can't believe it!" He looks back toward Cana. "Jesus healed him when He said the words!"

Now, returning to the text, things begin to make sense. We modern readers have seen the movie. We know Jesus healed the boy when He pronounced the words, "Your son will live." But the royal official had no reason to think that. He'd thought the words were prophetic, but he knew then that they were power. It was then, and only then, that this royal official with a Jewish upbringing believed. Why then? Because for any Jew with even nominal faith, one distinguishing characteristic set the true God apart from all other pretenders to the universal throne: our God causes things to happen by the power of His words.

I can almost hear the father putting two and two together. "The true God said 'Let there be light' and there was light. Yesterday at one o'clock Jesus said, 'Your son will live,' and my son lived." At that moment—and it could not have been until that moment—the father realized Jesus' identity as the Son of God not just a prophet of God, and he believed.

PERFORMATIVE WORDS

Now that we have created the timeline and discovered what it reveals, let's back up from the story and collect ourselves. I'm almost breathless myself! This miracle unveils something we moderns hardly appreciate. The greatest demonstration of God's deity is His ability to create everything by the power of His word. That's who He is. That's what He does. His words are not just informative; they are performative. Divine words spoken long-distance from over eighteen miles away had caused the terminally sick boy to recover.

We must adopt a higher view of the Word of God than we often do. We need to approach the Bible believing it is more than a repository of accurate and authoritative information. It is that, of course. But too often we stop there. We milk its instruction, principles, precepts, and eternally true information for all they're worth and try to live according to them. That's right and good. But God's Word is more than that. God's words perform His will.

It has always been that way, and so it shall remain. God's words cause everything that counts. God's words created everything (Gen. 1) and sustain everything (Heb. 1:2–3). He is not a grand watchmaker, as the deists claim, who created the material universe that now functions by fixed laws independent of His faithful involvement. If He ever was to stop speaking His will for this universe to exist, at that very moment everything would stop existing.

God's words always accomplish His purposes (Isa. 55:10–11). His words create faith (Rom. 10:17) and cause spiritual rebirth (1 Pet. 1:23). They discern and expose our inner thoughts (Heb. 4:12). They cleanse (Eph. 5:25–26) and sanctify (John 17:17). His words can be in us so we bear much fruit (John 15:7–8). And thankfully, His words defeat the Enemy of our souls (Eph. 6:17).

One day my wife and I received a phone call about a thirtysomething lady who, although a devoted Christian, suffered frequent bouts of depression and spiritual attack as a result of her childhood exposure to her parents' and grandparents' satanic practices, including human sacrifice. She needed help breaking free from recurring, debilitating torment, so we arranged to meet with her. We followed no preconceived formula—indeed we had never encountered anything like this before. My wife felt strongly impressed prior to our session to use a specific psalm at a key moment and asked the lady to read it aloud through her empty eyes. As she did, an oppressive, almost visible cloud of sadness lifted. Her torment immediately departed, but the proof of her freedom played out over the years of a stable life of peace and joy.

Experiences like that of the royal official and this tormented woman have a way of helping us know what happened in the first moments of time.

God spoke. He still speaks, and good things happen.

20/20 FOCUS

1. Can you give an example of another occasion when Jesus caused something miraculous to happen by simply speaking words?

2. Reflect on the difference between the royal official taking Jesus at His word and his eventual believing in Jesus. Though he didn't initially grasp Jesus' identity, ponder how trust in Jesus begins as seeing Him as One who gives accurate and authoritative information. Could you do a better job of taking Jesus at His word? How so?

3. Consider two ways to approach God's Word: as *informative* (gives accurate life information) or *performative* (causes God's will to happen).

How do you tend to relate to Scripture most often? How might you relate more effectively to God's Word as performative?

4. What Scripture might you pray performatively?

Lord, I know my words have no power in themselves, but Yours do. I want to take more seriously the potential I have for effective prayer and ministry. Help me trust and employ the performative nature of Your words as provided in Scripture. You promised if I remain in You and Your words in me, I can ask whatever I wish and it will be given (John 15:7). Show me more about how to live in that promise. Amen.

VISION CHECK

Creating an accurate timeline is often difficult, as biblical narratives compress time, so we miss the actual time frame involved. It's important to walk through a story "stretching out" the events to their full length.

Read the story in Acts 12 of the apostle Peter's miraculous release from prison. You will find this vague verse: "So Peter was kept in prison, but the church was earnestly praying to

God for him" (v. 5). There is no clue how long the church prayed before Peter was released. Imagine their prayer gatherings and how long they might have waited, given their disbelief when they were told Peter was at the front door. Write down your ideas and compare them with those shared on dougnewton.com or the Fresh Eyes app.

3

DAYWORKERS

Peter Healing the Lame Man
Acts 3:1–11

Would you stand on your head in a
local convenience store if it meant
someone might be saved?

What gets you out of bed in the morning? This question is commonly asked in job interviews these days. Potential employers are not looking for smart-aleck replies like "The alarm clock" or "The smell of coffee" or "My noisy kids." They hope to hear what motivates you in your daily tasks. Nondiscretionary obligations make up 90 percent of life. We must work, eat, pay bills, go grocery shopping, take care of the kids, mow the grass, wash clothes, maintain the car, etcetera. And the etceteras keep etcetering. Interviewers know that. They want to know whether you, as Henry David Thoreau expressed in his classic book *Walden*, are trying to "live deep and suck out all the marrow of life"[1] instead of letting life suck all the marrow out of you. What moves you?

Unfortunately, many people do not have a good answer. We would like to think Christian believers are uniquely blessed with motivation. After all, Jesus promised us an abundant life of purpose, joy, and camaraderie. The sad fact is, however, many Christians are sad. They may not be suffering from clinical depression (though some are), but they still live with nagging feelings of depression.

Many things can cause this common malaise, one being a lack of meaning. Human beings, created in God's image, are wired to work with God. The apostle Paul affirmed that fact when he wrote, "For we are God's handiwork, created in Christ Jesus to do good works, which God prepared in advance for us to do" (Eph. 2:10). Jesus identified a paradox of the kingdom when He promised that reinvigorating soul rest would result from working in tandem with Him. "Take my yoke upon you and learn from me," He said, "for I am gentle and humble in heart, and you will find rest for your souls" (Matt. 11:29).

It stands to reason, then, that we human beings suffer intrusive anxiety and emotional inertia when we lack a sense of divine purpose, one that gives meaning to all our activities, both discretionary and nondiscretionary. No prescription or brief high can bring the satisfying peace and joy divine partnership brings.

Many studies over the years have demonstrated the benefit of meaningful work as an effective antidote to depression. How much more effective that work can be when it occurs alongside the One who designed you to join in His work.

What gets you up in the morning? To see how Jesus wants to use you that day is a pretty good answer and a better stimulant than caffeine. But is that your answer? And is that really how it works? Can we—should we—expect to have a sense of daily employment with the Lord? Are we to live like dayworkers, waiting for the Lord to drive up and take us into the harvest field every morning?

Let's go to a wonderful, well-known miracle the Spirit of Jesus performed through Peter and John for some insight into these questions: the healing of the lame man (Acts 3:1–11). We'll look at it with fresh eyes, and the insight will come when we eventually notice two often-overlooked words.

THE SIGNIFICANCE OF "EVERY DAY"

A man, crippled all his life, legs tucked motionless under him, sat right at the entrance to the temple—the gate called Beautiful. Someone carried him there every day. Acts records why, saying, "Now a man who was lame from birth was being carried to the temple gate called Beautiful, where he was put every day to beg from those going into the temple courts" (3:2).

Because he was crippled from birth and was now over forty years old (4:22), he probably had seniority among beggars and perhaps could lay claim to prime real estate for begging. Everyone entering the temple for prayer was motivated to do one last act of almsgiving to get on God's good side just before praying.

So he was hopeful when Peter and John stopped—he didn't know they were *the* Peter and John—and asked him to look up from his beggar's habit of lowering his gaze and make eye contact. He thought, *All right! Someone's going to make a show of their giving.* (We know from Jesus' critique of the Pharisees that they were prone to prideful charity.)

So the man looked up but heard a very disappointing opening line from Peter: "Silver *or* gold I do not have …"

He probably thought, *Oh great. You have no money—plus, you have a very strange way of saying it.* "Silver or gold I do not have. Silver or gold I do not have."

"… but what I do have I give you …"

Oh great … What? Are you going to give me a little "God loves you" sticker?

"In the name of Jesus Christ of Nazareth, walk" (3:6).

You probably know what happened next. He did just that. This guy who had never stood upright in his life, whose point of view was always staring up into people's nostrils, suddenly looked another human being eye to eye. It took just a moment for the liquid in his inner ear to slosh around and for him to find his balance, but then he took his first step, something his parents had waited forty years to see. Probably because he watched with envy all those years as people walked past him, he had studied the motion and imagined doing it himself. So it took him only a minute to mimic that image and begin walking, then running, then jumping and praising God!

But here's the question: Why did Peter stop and offer him healing on that particular day? Luke specifically said the man was placed there "every day" to beg and everyone recognized him as the one who always sat outside the gate. That phrase "every day" gets overlooked, but it is very significant. For Luke told us in the previous chapter that the disciples went to pray "every day" at the temple (Acts 2:46). That means day after day they walked right past the man and did nothing. Why on this day did they stop?

THE SCANNER

I think the explanation that best fits the text is the Spirit of Jesus gave them a direct instruction. How can I be so sure? Maybe on other days Peter and John were caught up in conversation, or other things occupied their minds, so they walked past without noticing. That happens to us all the time. We stride right past human needs all around us. Then, occasionally, we aren't so preoccupied and happen to notice. So maybe on this day Peter just happened to notice the guy and had a moment of sympathy. Why not *that* explanation? Because moments of sympathy don't produce such extreme confidence.

Look at Peter's actions after telling the lame man to get up and walk, and notice the order of the verbs: "*Taking* him by the right hand, he *helped* him up, and instantly the man's feet and ankles *became* strong. He *jumped* to his feet and *began* to walk" (3:7–8).

Peter commanded him to walk, then reached down to take him by the right hand and help him up *before* he saw any evidence of healing. Peter didn't command him to walk but then ask a diagnostic question: "Are you feeling any tingling in your legs?" He was so sure of the man's healing that he reached down and pulled him up. Only then, according to the text, did the man's legs and feet become instantly strong. Only some direct instruction from God's Spirit could have persuaded Peter to risk lifting up the crippled man *before* seeing any evidence of healing.

Perhaps we wouldn't interpret Peter's experience this way so quickly had we not read about a parallel experience Jesus had that provides a helpful precedent. In John 5, Jesus entered a hospital-like setting of infirm people gathered around a pool of water thought to occasionally provide therapeutic benefits. Apparently, people believed angels invisibly stirred the water from time to time and whoever entered the water first was healed.

Rather than offering His healing powers to everyone there, Jesus approached only one person (which was out of character for Jesus) and initiated a conversation that led to the man's healing. The similarities between this miracle and Peter's miracle are striking: this man was also crippled for nearly forty years; Jesus, like Peter, offered healing without the man asking; and Jesus similarly commanded the man to get up and walk. Later when the Jews asked Jesus to defend His Sabbath-breaking act of healing the man, Jesus explained: "Very truly I tell you, the Son can do nothing by himself; he can do only what he sees his Father doing, because whatever the Father does the Son also does" (v. 19).

In short, Jesus claimed to be acting from an ability to perceive spiritually His heavenly Father's will and activity. Probably that acute sensitivity resulted from His daily regimen of prayerful communion with the Father. Peter and the other apostles were also following that regimen, according to Luke's description of their lifestyle post-Pentecost. Luke said, "They devoted themselves to the apostles' teaching and to fellowship, to the breaking of bread and to prayer" (Acts 2:42).

These disciples who, as far as Scripture records, never asked Jesus to teach them to heal or preach or cast out demons but made only one educational request—"Teach us to pray" (Luke 11:1)—demonstrated that Jesus' example of daily prayer had penetrated their hearts and rearranged their priorities. So it is no wonder and makes great sense, given the parallels between the two healings, that Peter was similarly perceptive of the Spirit's spontaneous instruction on that particular day.

I wonder whether an expectation that the Spirit might instruct at any moment was the norm for the early believers. Think about deacon Philip in Acts, who got his start in ministry helping organize the food distribution for Greek widows within the church (6:5). His spiritual gifts and ministry skills apparently expanded to the point that he became a dynamic evangelist when the gospel spread beyond his home church in Jerusalem. Acts 8 records him having an experience of spiritual instruction. It states, "Now an angel of the Lord said to Philip, 'Go south to the road—the desert road—that goes down from Jerusalem to Gaza.' So he started out, and on his way he met an Ethiopian eunuch, an important official in charge of all the treasury of the Kandake (which means 'queen of the Ethiopians'). This man had gone to Jerusalem to worship, and on his way home was sitting in his chariot reading the Book of Isaiah the prophet. The Spirit told Philip, 'Go to that chariot and stay near it'" (vv. 26–29).

The timing was perfect, as only the Holy Spirit could have known, for the eunuch to encounter someone who could lead him to faith in Jesus. So the Spirit dispatched Philip on the spur of the moment, and as soon as the evangelistic encounter bore fruit, Philip was transported away by the Spirit just as spontaneously (v. 39).

Remarkable.

I'm not sure who, but sometime in Christian history someone decided to make most of us believe that spontaneous ministry instructions simply don't happen today, at least not as a general rule. Whoever it was convinced us to relegate such experiences to the class of "rare exceptions." Based on what argument, I don't know. The fact that it rarely happens? Just because most people do not forgive offenders seventy times seven does not mean it is an invalid expectation and should not be a common experience for all Christians.

I am not saying a person receives spontaneous ministry instructions from the Lord every day. Yet people who stay in prayerful communion with the Lord and who believe He may occasionally give specific ministry instructions are likely to receive those instructions quite frequently, because they stay "tuned in." It's like living with a police scanner turned on.

I can bear witness to this fact and have many stories to tell. Like the time I was spiritually "informed" to travel to a distant city to lead a man I didn't know out of the sin of adultery. When I obeyed, with an understandable amount of trepidation, it turned out he had just prayed that morning for God to send him "a Nathan" (the prophet who confronted King David about his sin of adultery with Bathsheba in 2 Sam. 12:7) to help deliver him from that sin. Like David, the fellow I sought out was set free from his sin and found forgiveness. His marriage and family were saved from destruction, and he became a friend and coworker for many years.

Stories like this abound throughout Christendom today. Like the time God's Spirit told a woman to leave a church meeting and turn out of the church parking lot in the opposite direction from her route home. Not knowing why or where she should go, she sensed that she should pull into a local convenience store. When she entered, the craziest thought struck her mind: *Go up to the cashier and stand on your head.* More than likely, most of us would have stopped right there and rushed home. But she did it! The cashier burst into tears and explained how despondent he had been about life and how he had just told God that evening, "If You're real, have someone come in here and stand on their head in front of me."

I'm not suggesting you start practicing headstands. But why not move as close as you can to the Lord every day? The world is no less full today than in Bible times of people who desperately need to know God is real and His compassion is incredible. Why wouldn't God want to dispatch His people like you and me far and wide and often to prove His love and offer His grace? Most of the time we can probably offer that love and grace without special instructions. The Bible does a great job showing us how to do that in general terms. But there will be times, many more than we think, when God wants to give us the joy of offering His love in just the right way at just the right time with just the right words. What a privilege when you get to be part of that partnership.

That will get anyone out of bed in the morning!

20/20 FOCUS

1. Considering a person's sense of meaning comes largely from engaging day-to-day in God's purposes, on a scale of one to ten (with ten being very meaningful), how meaningful does your

life feel currently? Why did you assign that number?

2. The chapter's key point is based on the assumption that Peter and John passed by the lame man frequently, an assumption supported by the use of "every day" in Acts 2:46 and 3:2. What other repeated phrase in those same verses supports that main assumption? And why?

3. God occasionally wants to employ us in His work by giving specific instructions. But most Christians hesitate to act because they doubt their ability to hear God accurately. What might we do to avoid the problems of hesitation or false impressions?

4. Can you think of a time you acted on a "sense" of a divine instruction? Or maybe a time you chickened out? (We all do it.)

Lord, I certainly don't want to be arrogant or presumptuous about my ability to hear from You. But I am convinced You want to employ me in Your work and occasionally give me specific

instructions. I am open. Guide me. Guard me.
Use me. I want my days to count for You. Amen.

VISION CHECK

Little kids possess an insatiable need to ask the question "Why?"
That question was the key to the insights in this chapter. You'll
be surprised at what you might discover when you rekindle that
childlike habit. Why did Jesus or the disciples or some other
character do what they did? Why then? Why that way? (Though
this requires imagination and speculation, start with clues the
text/context provides and the Bible as a whole supports.)

Go to another story of Jesus healing a lame man: John 5. Jot
down the basic facts and then start asking why about everything
that transpired. Don't forget to read the immediate context
before and after the healing. See what new insights come to
your mind. Then hop on dougnewton.com or the Fresh Eyes
app to compare your thoughts with mine.

4

FISH SANDWICHES

Feeding the Five Thousand

Mark 6:30–44

How did five loaves and two fish feed
over ten thousand rather than just ten?

Whether you're talking about money, time, energy, or resources of any sort, people never think they have enough. This is not usually a function of greed, however. Maybe poor choices. Or overcommitment. But most people who wish they had more time and money truly are a day late and a dollar short. They need more, because they don't have enough to cover their current obligations.

I can hear the blamers: "They got themselves into that mess. Buying stuff on credit. Signing their kids up for ten different sports. They just need to slow down. Discipline their spending. Live within their means."

Yeah … well, lots of problems are caused by unfortunate circumstances. But okay, we got it. People can get themselves into a mess too. Nevertheless, they still are time and money crunched, and all you've done is criticize. Is that the way God looks at people in debt up to their eyeballs? "You've made your bed; now lie in it."

No. He has compassion on—especially on—the plight of people who made their own mess. Isn't that, in fact, the very heart of the cross of Jesus Christ? God saves those who chose their way into calamity.

In the Old Testament, the Lord revealed exhibit A of His brand of compassion when He established the Jubilee system. Every seven years people who had racked up debts had those debts forgiven, and every fifty years any property people might have forfeited was restored to them. No questions asked. They were not brought before an examiner to explain how they got into such debt and to justify why they deserved another chance at landownership and financial stability. The Lord was so adamant about this spirit of compassion toward those who suffered lack that He considered it evil to withhold help, even if it meant the helper might pay a personal price.

> At the end of every seven years you must cancel debts. This is how it is to be done: Every creditor shall cancel any loan they have made to a fellow Israelite. They shall not require payment from anyone among their own people, because the LORD's time for canceling debts has been proclaimed....
>
> If anyone is poor among your fellow Israelites in any of the towns of the land the LORD your God is giving you, do not be hardhearted or tightfisted toward them. Rather, be openhanded and freely lend them whatever

they need. *Be careful not to harbor this wicked thought: "The seventh year, the year for canceling debts, is near," so that you do not show ill will toward the needy among your fellow Israelites and give them nothing.* (Deut. 15:1–2, 7–9)

Most Christians understand this idea of compassion. We aren't blamers. We want to do something to help. This spirit of compassion motivates every Christian ministry on earth: to help those who can't help themselves. But we encounter a chronic problem here. We, the people in compassion ministries, are among those trapped in lack. We face multitudes of needs with inadequate resources. We who minister to beggars become beggars. We are full of mercy but starved of means.

Is it inevitable that our compassion will always be a day late and a dollar short? Not according to the apostle Paul's promise in 2 Corinthians when he was raising funds for Jerusalem's poverty-stricken Christians. He wrote, "And God is able to bless you abundantly, so that in all things at all times, having all that you need, you will abound in every good work" (9:8).

Paul was so certain of this "abundance principle" that he repeated it even more explicitly just two verses later: "Now he who supplies seed to the sower and bread for food will also supply and increase your store of seed and will enlarge the harvest of your righteousness. You will be enriched in every way so that you can be generous on every occasion" (vv. 10–11).

That's a wonderfully encouraging promise for those who long to be compassionate and generous. If only it were true …

Well, of course it is true, but the collective experience of most Christian ministries doesn't appear to verify it. So the question is: Why? If God enriches us in every way, if He makes all grace abound to us who intend to do good works, so we always have all we need, why isn't that our reality? In all things at all times, having less than we need, we barely get by doing less than all the good work that needs to get done. That's more like our experience.

I think there's an explanation for our chronically under-resourced ministries—in Jesus' miracle of the feeding of the five thousand, if we examine it with fresh eyes. Let's review the story as it is told in Mark 6:30–44. The key to seeing this miracle with fresh eyes is to put yourself in the disciples' position in every scene.

SCENE ONE: MINISTRY REPORTS

The story opens with the disciples gathered around Jesus and reporting "all they had done and taught" (v. 30). They had just returned from their first ministry trip without Him. A few days prior He had tossed them the keys to the church van, told them to go do the stuff they had seen Him doing, and then surprised them by not getting into the van.

Totally on their own, they ventured out, looked at their WWJD bracelets, and began plotting their approach, finally agreeing Jesus would travel around and see what happens that draws a crowd. So that's what they did, apparently, and sure enough, things happened. Wonderful things. They healed people. They cast out demons. And not just a few times either. Numerous times. They participated in so many miraculous encounters that reporting them all took hours. (What a stark contrast to testimony services in most of our churches today!) We know this because "so many people were coming and going that they did not even have a chance to eat" (v. 31). Remember that fact. It will be important later.

The scene closes with Jesus recognizing that the disciples were like kids coming home from youth camp, running on a spiritual high. So He suggested they take a breath, slow down, and get away from the bustling limelight for a little while to be alone with Him. They shoved a boat off into waist-deep water, hopped in, caught a good breeze, and sailed for the opposite shore.

SCENE TWO: A HUNGRY, HELPLESS MULTITUDE

After about an hour or so, they neared the lake's northern shore and were surprised to see a crowd of people greeting them with cheers, flapping robes, and clouds of dust. Perhaps the people on the shore were so enthused by the disciples' testimonies they could not bear missing out on more stories. So they trekked around the lake's north shore, spreading the word and picking up more fans along the way until thousands of eager people mobbed the beach.

This was probably the disciples' first experience of being the center of attention. It might have felt good initially, but they were certainly glad to pass the ministry baton to Jesus when He saw the spiritually hungry crowd and decided to feed their souls rather than continue on with the retreat plans.

As time wore on, however, the famished disciples started to fidget. They gazed at a tired sun beginning to settle down for the evening, then waited for Jesus to pause and pulled Him aside. Doing their best to hide any sign of selfish motives, they couched their comments in apparent concern for the crowd: "It's already very late. Send the people away so that they can go to the surrounding countryside and villages and buy themselves something to eat" (Mark 6:35–36). What they probably meant was, "Jesus, can You wrap it up so we can eat?"

SCENE THREE: CONFOUNDING COMMANDS

Here's where things went weird. Jesus gave hungry disciples an unrealistic command: "You give them something to eat" (Mark 6:37).

What were the disciples to think? Of course they assumed the only way to fulfill that command was to purchase food. That's the mode their minds were in, because they had just suggested that the people be sent away to "buy" food.

We don't know how much time elapsed between Jesus' command that the disciples provide food for the multitude and their response. But according to Scripture, "They said to him, 'That would take more than half a year's wages! Are we to go and spend that much on bread and give it to them to eat?'" (v. 37).

Even though the text jumps quickly from command to response, it couldn't have been immediate. Perhaps they clustered off to the side, deliberating like a church finance committee. How much would that cost? Matthew, the former tax collector, was probably good with figures. "How many people do you suppose are out there?" he asked. That calculation alone probably took a few minutes, as they counted a group of one hundred people, noted its approximate size, imagined the multitude in sections, estimated the number of groups, and multiplied. Good thing Matthew kept his abacus!

Somehow these men, who rarely shopped for groceries, arrived at a price per person for a basic meal—who knows whether they were even close to right—and multiplied that figure times the estimated size of the multitude. Thirty thousand dollars, by modern equivalent!

Something like that must have occurred before they returned to Jesus in mild protest. But I think something else

probably happened before that. Their protest implies they recognized the command to be unreasonable. Remember, these
men were inclined to obey Jesus. They probably wouldn't have
refused without first attempting to comply. Did they brain-
storm for a few moments about a fund-raising campaign? Did
one of them suggest they distribute pledge cards throughout
the crowd, maybe even ask Bartholomew, who had a beautiful
baritone voice, to sing an emotional song before having Peter
make a stirring appeal? Was this the first time in human history
when someone proposed the idea of creating a poster with a
big thermometer marked with the thirty-thousand-dollar goal
at the top so they could track their progress?

Whatever they considered and for however long they tried,
no plan seemed realistic. Jesus just doesn't understand finances,
they concluded. He thinks you can just pull money out of the
mouth of a fish! So they reluctantly but firmly brought their
findings to Jesus. "Can't be done. No way."

However, Jesus didn't even blink when they balked. He
knew what they would think, so He was ready with the next
command: "How many loaves do you have?… Go and see"
(Mark 6:38).

Again the text jumps abruptly to their response: "Five—and
two fish." Please notice, just as we did, before that something
probably went on between Jesus' command and their response.
However, instead of considering that right now, we'll come back
to it in a minute.

SCENE FOUR: A MIRACLE IN THEIR HANDS

What happens next is well-known, of course, just poorly imagined. Yes, we picture Jesus directing the disciples to seat the people in groups of hundreds and fifties (vv. 39–40). Their previous feasibility study prepared them for that task. We picture Jesus holding a loaf of bread in His hands, looking up to heaven to give thanks, breaking it in sections—easy to picture because we see something like that every time we observe Holy Communion—and handing chunks to each of His disciples for distribution (v. 41).

Here's where our imaginations usually stop short. So let's press on. Imagine one of the disciples receiving his chunk of bread, then looking at the first group of fifty. Imagine his brows crinkling with the question, "How is this chunk going to feed even these fifty people, much less all the other groups in my section?"

He would have been tempted to break off for each person a piece the size of a Communion wafer, thinking he would have to stretch the bread as far as possible. "At least we can give each person a little taste," he could have said. But that approach wouldn't have made sense. Jesus talked about feeding hungry people. A wafer of bread would not begin to satiate their hunger. So when the disciple came to his first person, I imagine him boldly deciding to offer a piece of bread that had a chance of helping ease the rumbling of an empty stomach.

Now imagine this: he broke off a good-sized piece, probably thinking, *Only about three people will eat before I run out*, handed it to a grateful person, who received and relished it. But as he did that, he felt movement in his hands, looked down, and the broken-off piece had grown back on the loaf. *What? Look at that! Ha! I can't believe it!* So he proceeded to the next person and did the same thing. Broke off a piece—a little larger one this time—testing a nascent hypothesis forming in his mind. He handed it to the person and—*voila!*—that piece grew back. He not only felt it; he also saw it happen this time, because he was watching to see what it would look like. And all the disciples experienced this!

Can you imagine the exploding excitement the disciples felt? To hold a miracle happening in their hands! You know how the miracle ended. The whole crowd was well fed, and the leftovers filled a basket for each of the hungry disciples.

This is a remarkable story, one that stretches our imagination and credulity. But that's how it must have happened. Jesus not only fed the whole multitude by turning meager resources into megaresources, but He also blessed the disciples with the privilege of participating in the discovery and delivery of plenty. How we wish our churches and ministries would have that kind of experience. But as we acknowledged at the beginning of this chapter, that generally isn't the way it happens. Why must our compassionate hearts be tormented with visions of longing multitudes and lagging resources? For a possible answer, let's backtrack to scene three and that moment when Jesus invited the disciples to see how many loaves they could offer.

SCENE THREE REVISITED

Here's what I find remarkable, given what I know about myself. If I had been in that situation and Jesus had told me to check how many loaves and fish I had to offer, it's highly likely I would have counted five loaves and two fish. But feeling my own hunger pangs, I would have made myself a quick fish sandwich, secretly wolfed it down behind a big rock, and come back to Jesus saying, "I have four loaves and one fish," with the smell of sardines on my breath!

I'm just being honest. And if I had been there and done that, I think only nine or ten people—tops—would have been fed that day. The great majority of the multitude would have gone hungry. Of course, we can't know for sure, because that's not what the disciples did. However, I think the working of God's generous grace and provision gets interrupted if and when His followers use their resources to care for themselves first and offer only the excess to God.

When the Lord tells us to go see what we have to offer, whether regarding time, talents, or treasure, He expects us to declare everything we have—not everything we have *left over* after we have cared for ourselves. In contrast to my tendency, the actual disciples displayed a paradox of kingdom economics that memorable day. They gave away what they themselves needed, and Jesus turned their sacrifice into surplus.

In the days after Pentecost, when God's Spirit moved across the face of the world and created by His living Word the first church ever, we glimpse what He wanted the church to be like before people started messing with it. Clearly, His generous Spirit desired to create—and did in fact create—people who were radically generous (Acts 2:44–45). They clung to nothing (4:32). They placed everything in the Lord's hands to meet people's needs (vv. 34–35).

Could it be that anything less than that kind of generosity grieves the Lord and stifles His miraculous provision? Could it be that our resources fall short of the divinely promised "having all that you need" because our breath smells like sardines?

Miracles of surplus follow moments of radical sacrifice.

20/20 FOCUS

1. Give away what we ourselves need? That's counterintuitive. Can you think of any other counterintuitive commands of Jesus?

2. The nightly news often features stories of *common* generosity. But have you ever seen examples of *radical* generosity where people jeopardized their own well-being for the sake of giving to others? Describe one.

3. The apostle Paul described a case of radical generosity in 2 Corinthians 8:1–3. Review how and why he commended the Macedonians.

Lord, I freely admit that everything in me is geared toward making sure I have what I and my loved ones need before I even think of giving anything away, whether resources, time, or effort. And I can see how that can cut me off from experiencing evidence of Your gracious provision. Give me courage and faith to move toward a lifestyle of radical generosity. Amen.

VISION CHECK

Years ago, it was popular for Christians to wear WWJD bracelets to remind them to behave properly by asking "What Would Jesus Do?" That's always a good practice, of course, but to have fresh eyes on biblical narratives, consider wearing a different reminder: "What Would I Do (in that situation)?"

Although cultures have changed over time, human beings haven't. How would you have felt under those circumstances? What would your reactions have been? It's generally safe to assume that the story's characters would have dealt with the same kinds of thoughts and feelings you would have in their place.

Practice putting yourself into Gideon's story (Judg. 7), when God told him to whittle down his army to 300 soldiers before launching battle against 135,000 Midianite soldiers. What *doesn't* the text say that you can reasonably assume occurred in Gideon's mind? Does that give you any new insights about the nature of obedience? Hop on dougnewton.com or the Fresh Eyes app to compare your thoughts with mine.

DEAD PIGS

Exorcising the Demoniac

Mark 5:1–20

"How can I be sure of what I believe?" is
a question we all ask. Will God answer?

Does Jesus really answer our prayers for a good parking space? Or to find a "just right" dress on a 75-percent-off clearance rack? I've heard those kinds of testimonies—healing common headaches, car accidents that almost but didn't happen—often with a twinge of skepticism and concern, because there are usually people listening in the same room who suffer with multiyear, unrelenting, debilitating headaches or whose son or daughter died in a car crash.

Don't get me wrong. I want to give God all the credit He deserves. I have no doubt God wonderfully intervenes in answer to prayer and many times before we've even prayed. But, for example, does He really orchestrate our worship services in ways we sometimes claim? "Did you see how the last song fit the sermon perfectly? The song leader who picked it had no idea what the preacher was going to be preaching!"

Well, if we're going to give God credit for those situations, then we had better go all the way and give Him credit for this one too …

I was preaching a sermon series on Galatians. One particular Sunday I planned to exposit the part where Paul was angry with the Judaizers for distorting the gospel of salvation by faith and insisting that Gentile converts be circumcised. My practice was to have a lay leader read aloud the upcoming sermon's text. So I asked him to read up to the point where Paul shouts through his pen, "I wish they would go the whole way and emasculate themselves!" (Gal. 5:12).

The lay leader hesitated. "You're not serious?"

"Yes. In fact, read it like you're angry. Really emphasize it." He did not want to do it, but he was a team player.

In those days our practice was to insert a moment of special music—a solo, duet, or instrumental—between the Scripture reading and the sermon. So the time came for the Scripture reading. Nervously, the lay leader began, but he valiantly pressed on to the punch line, gave it everything he had, and rang out the "emasculate themselves!" beautifully.

Seamlessly the piano played the opening notes of the special music, and without introduction our soloist, a petite college girl who was the poster child of innocence, stepped to the microphone and sang the wistful opening line, "I'll never be the same again …"

The sanctuary erupted in laughter. She didn't get it and sang on. Someone explained it to her later.

Shouldn't we credit God for that perfectly orchestrated serendipity too? Maybe it didn't feed any souls, but if laughter is the best medicine, it certainly healed multitudes that morning.

Trying to figure why, when, and how God chooses to grant our prayers is more challenging than calculus. At least there we have equations. Has anyone ever discovered an elegant (as mathematicians say) prayer equation?

The answer is no. We are simply left in a conundrum. This story of the exorcising of the demoniac doesn't appear to help either. For as we shall see, Jesus received two main requests in this episode: one from the emancipated demoniac who wanted to follow Jesus for the rest of his life, and one from the legion of tormenting demons. Guess whose request Jesus granted? Not his brand-new disciple's but the demons'! See what I mean? A conundrum.

EXPLORING THE CONUNDRUM

Let's review. Here is the former demoniac's request: "As Jesus was getting into the boat, the man who had been demon-possessed begged to go with him" (Mark 5:18).

He was pleading. I picture him at Jesus' feet. "Please, please, please, let me go with You." If that isn't a heartfelt prayer, I don't know what is. Prayer is often nothing more than presenting our requests with thanksgiving (Phil. 4:6), and what the man did definitely qualifies. True, Jesus stood right there with him in person and not "up in heaven" as we picture Him today when we pray. But in every respect the newly restored man's words were a passionate prayer request—and one that came from a thankful convert. Why wouldn't Jesus answer that prayer?

That's a question made more troubling when contrasted with the request Jesus did answer. In similar fashion the demons threw the man at Jesus' feet and cried, "Please, please, please, don't torture us!" The heartfelt petition continued: "He begged Jesus again and again not to send them out of the area. A large herd of pigs was feeding on the nearby hillside. The demons begged Jesus, 'Send us among the pigs; allow us to go into them'" (Mark 5:10–12).

The Greek word for "beg" is *parakaleo*, from which we get one of our words for the Holy Spirit—the *Paraclete*—because He is the one whom we passionately seek and who lovingly helps in our time of need. Is that not the nature of prayer?

So the legion of demons voiced their "prayer request" through the enemy-occupied man's larynx, pleading for Jesus' mercy. Bible teachers offer various explanations for their desire not to be geographically displaced. Some assert that demons function within assigned regions and territories. That may or may not be the case. What is troubling, however, and further whirls the swirling conundrum, is the fact that Jesus not only said yes to this prayer but did so at the expense of two thousand pigs and the economic and emotional equilibrium of the pigs' owners and townspeople. "He gave them permission, and the impure spirits came out and went into the pigs. The herd, about two thousand in number, rushed down the steep bank into the lake and were drowned. Those tending the pigs ran off and reported this in the town and countryside.... Those who had seen it told the people what had happened to the demon-possessed man—and told about the pigs as well. Then the people began to plead with Jesus to leave their region" (vv. 13–14, 16–17).

So why did Jesus deny the prayer of His new convert but grant the request of the demons?

EXPLAINING THE CONUNDRUM

We find the answer by noting Jesus' instruction to the former demoniac and empathizing with a handful of people we hardly notice but for whom Jesus showed special concern: the man's family. "Jesus did not let him, but said, 'Go home to your own people and tell them how much the Lord has done for you, and how he has had mercy on you.' So the man went away and began to tell in the Decapolis how much Jesus had done for him. And all the people were amazed" (vv. 19–20).

When Jesus refused to grant the man's request to go with Him, He redirected the former demoniac's attention homeward. We don't know anything about the man's family, but he probably had a wife and children. Why would this be significant?

Think about his wife. Put yourself in her position. Was he a demoniac when she originally married him? This chapter describes him as someone living among the tombs of the dead: "No one could bind him anymore, not even with a chain. For he had often been chained hand and foot, but he tore the chains apart and broke the irons on his feet. No one was strong enough to subdue him. Night and day among the tombs and in the hills he would cry out and cut himself with stones" (Mark 5:3–5).

Was he that kind of man when they married? Did she walk near the local cemetery one day, hear his insane screaming, find herself attracted, run home, buy a bride's magazine, and start planning her wedding? "Oh, Mother, I've just met the most wonderful man! I can't wait to marry him." Of course not.

Even if her parents arranged the marriage, which is likely, they would not have chosen a crazy man for a son-in-law and the father of their grandchildren. Somewhere along the way in the marriage, something began to change in him. Perhaps one day he threw a fit. His irrational behavior escalated. His anger grew more and more frightening. Too often she had to gather the children together and run from the house. Her life had become a nightmare.

Nothing helped. Not trying to be a better wife. Love him more. Pray for him. Eventually her parents intervened. Took her and the kids back into the protection of their home. Perhaps that sent her husband over the edge. He went berserk, and the whole town had to step in to drive him away, or there was no telling what he might do.

Maybe it didn't happen exactly that way. But something similar must have happened. Young girls don't marry demoniacs or overt abusers who turn home into hell. Her life had become a story she never could have imagined. As much as it wounded her spirit to hear him screaming at night in the hollows of the tombs, she was glad to be out of danger. Out of that marriage.

So what was she supposed to do? What was she supposed to think when he showed up on her doorstep "dressed and in his right mind" (v. 15) after Jesus delivered him from evil? Just believe him? How was she supposed to know he'd really changed? How was she supposed to believe *it* wouldn't come back—whatever *it* was? Her husband appeared normal at the time of their courtship and wedding. Then later, out of the blue, he became a monster. Something in him—a dark power that lay hidden—rose up unexpectedly and devoured him, her, and their home. How was she supposed to believe the same thing wouldn't happen again?

It would take more than his words: "Sweetheart. I'm not the man I was. I promise you'll never see me behave like that again. You don't have to worry." How many women have heard similar words over the centuries? How many women have felt like a fool when he lapsed into the same behavior a second, third … or tenth time?

What she needed was not words. She needed evidence. Evidence of finality. Actually, the newly restored man did too. They all—the man, the wife, the kids, the parents, the townspeople—needed something they could point to. "There. See that? It's over. Everything's going to be different now."

Enter—or I should say exit—two thousand squealing, frenzied pigs, bobbing and thrashing and growing silent in the churning waves, washing up waterlogged on shore. Heaps and heaps of useless pork. And Jesus said, "So does that help?" You better believe it helped! The conundrum is solved: the demons got what they wanted so the man and his family could get what they needed.

THE GIFT OF EVIDENCE

Perhaps the most fundamental doctrine of the Christian faith across the centuries is *sola fide*—faith alone. Salvation does not come by human effort. No number of good works can earn the gift of eternal life. But like a swollen river that breaches levies and floods towns, over the centuries the *sola fide* doctrine has overwhelmed conventional Christian thought. We think that everything is based only on faith and not just the gift of salvation. But nothing could be further from the truth.

Faith is a gift, and God is the giver. Often faith comes by hearing the Word of God, but most of the time He gives and strengthens faith through the presentation of evidence. From the skies above and the stars beyond that "pour forth speech" (Ps. 19:1–2) to an empty tomb and expired swine below, God reveals the glory of His holiness and handiwork through observable data.

God is in the business of making the incredible credible. Yes, He expects us to believe some unbelievable things, but the God who loves us supremely understands how the hardest things require the hardiest proof.

What could be harder to believe than the fact that you and I can be rescued from the power of sin and evil? While our plight might not be as graphic as the demoniac's, it is just as grave. The power of sin and evil from within controls us, as it controlled him. Paul addressed this with blunt pessimism in Romans. He wrote, "I know that good itself does not dwell in me, that is, in my sinful nature. For I have the desire to do what is good, but I cannot carry it out. For I do not do the good I want to do, but the evil I do not want to do—this I keep on doing" (7:18–19).

We may not be bouncing off the walls of rough-hewn tombs, but we are just as helpless to cast out the domineering power of sin and enter spiritual freedom. According to Paul, only deliverance will do. And deliverance is precisely what Paul declared. "What a wretched man I am! Who will rescue me from this body that is subject to death? Thanks be to God, who delivers me through Jesus Christ our Lord!… Therefore, there is now no condemnation for those who are in Christ Jesus, because through Christ Jesus the law of the Spirit who gives life has set you free from the law of sin and death" (7:24—8:2).

The demoniac's transformation was immediate. Mark offered this threefold description of his emancipated condition:

"When they came to Jesus, they saw the man who had been possessed by the legion of demons, sitting there, dressed and in his right mind" (Mark 5:15).

"Sitting there"—as opposed to writhing in inconsolable, self-mutilating torment. "Dressed"—as opposed to exhibiting shameful nakedness. "In his right mind"—as opposed to uttering bizarre rants. This threefold description parallels our spiritual change too closely for us to miss the correlation between what happened to him and what happens to us as we are transformed into people of peace, of righteousness, and with sound minds.

The point we must not miss, though, is that Jesus did not stop His transformative work. Even though profound initial evidence existed, that was not enough to reassure anyone—the man or his family—that the transformation was thorough and enduring. Everyone needed something more. Jesus graciously supplied that *something more* through the destruction of the pigs—undeniable evidence of evil power vanquished.

Evidence. This is what God loves to give.

By the time I was thirty-three, I had been preaching for nine years. All those years, I had to go through an informal ritual prior to every sermon. I reminded myself why I believed all this "Christianity stuff." I rehearsed five points methodically, literally counting to five on my fingers: the reliability of Scripture, the classic arguments for God's existence, the unquenchable witness of the early Christians in the face of persecution, the perseverance of the Christian witness across the centuries, and remarkable modern-day testimonies. Having reminded myself of my belief system's validity, I could step behind the pulpit one more Sunday.

But my intellectual process was like the Old Testament sacrificial system—something I had to repeat week after week in order to hold my faith firmly. I longed for something more. A surer, more lasting confidence. I told myself, *I shouldn't have to face these same questions and go through this ritual week after week.* So eventually I asked a small group of my congregation to pray for me as I went away to a ministry conference. "I need something to happen in my life to turn these question marks into exclamation points," I explained.

What happened is a long story for another time, but suffice it to say I longed for something, something which at that time I did not know God loves to give. At the very end of a four-day conference, a man approached me in a crowd of people. "You are wanting someone to pray for you, aren't you?" I said yes. Nothing else.

He laid his hand on my heart. When he did, my heart grew very warm, from the inside out. It was a strange sensation, not like the warmth of his hand on my chest. He said, "You've been desiring purity strongly." He could not have known I had been memorizing Psalm 51:10: "Create in me a pure heart, O God ..." My knees went weak. He continued, saying, "Sometime over the next two or three days the Lord will give you the desire of your heart, and you will begin to weep uncontrollably for several hours." Then he simply prayed a prayer of blessing. That was it.

Sure enough, partway through my five-hour trip home the next morning, I began to weep just as I decided to recite my Psalm 51:10 memory verse. I could not stop crying for the remaining three hours of the trip, even though I had to drive through two tollbooths on the interstate!

There were no dead pigs after that event, but the experience was so profound I was forever changed and convinced. As I write this chapter, I am sixty-three years old. Over the past thirty years, I have preached another fifteen hundred times. Not once since that experience have I ever had to use my five-finger recital of "Why I believe ..."

Since that moment, when I first understood God as the one who loves to give evidence to help us believe, I have had numerous opportunities to proclaim that fact and participate in evidentiary experiences that have reassured many others. (Although I am pleased to report that no animals have been harmed in the making of this testimony.)

20/20 FOCUS

1. Make a list of at least five biblical examples of what God did or does to help people believe something about Him or His promises.

2. A common saying is the only things certain in life are death and taxes. But is there anything else you would include in that list of things you are absolutely sure about? What enables you to be so convinced?

3. Many people struggle to believe in God's goodness and their value in His sight. When has something happened that helped you become more confident in God's love? How about in His acceptance? Or in your value?

4. The Bible does not continue the story, but in light of the way Jesus treated desperate people so compassionately in the gospel records, what might He have done for the poor herders who lost all their pigs?

Lord, sometimes I think the things that are most real are the hardest things to believe. I need Your help. Plus, there are things I once found easy to believe, but now they're not so easy. Would You help me believe? I will keep trying to believe what's true based on Your Word alone, knowing You'll give me the evidence I need in just the right way at just the right time as I stay focused on You. Amen.

VISION CHECK

It is common, when an author begins writing a novel, for him or her to develop the backstory. What led up to the point where the novel begins? How did the characters become who they are? What is the history of the place or situation they find themselves in? The full backstory, which never shows up in the novel, is important for everything that exists.

Similarly, all Bible miracles have a backstory, a real one. Sometimes the facts in the biblical account can help you imagine the backstory, which in turn helps you discover more truths in the miracle itself. For example, in John 9 the gospel writer offered several facts about a blind man and his parents that help us imagine their lives prior to the blind man's healing. Craft a simple backstory based on those facts that helps you identify with their situation before and after the healing. Then go to dougnewton.com or the Fresh Eyes app to compare your thoughts with mine.

6

TRAVEL PLANS

Calming the Storm

Mark 4:35—5:21

If you track the Lord's movements, you
can discover His priorities and join in.

If Neil Armstrong had not stepped foot on the moon, we might still be eating foil-covered TV dinners while watching grainy black-and-white *Dick Van Dyke* shows. The lunar landing was a great moment that changed history and our lives, but a great moment is never an isolated event. Most great moments in history are made up of minimoments. Like pieces of a jigsaw puzzle, they fit together to form a whole picture.

When Armstrong's boot touched *luna firma*, hundreds of significant advances in propulsion, computing, communication, materials science, and physiology had already occurred on *terra firma* to make that possible. Each of these individual achievements, notable and necessary in themselves, were most meaningful because they contributed to that one great accomplishment.

Our important advances in technology, including what makes your toaster toast and your refrigerator defrost, owe themselves to the systems developed during the Apollo program. There's no telling how many modern conveniences and advantages we might not have today if it weren't for NASA's quest.

Here's the point: when studying individual moments of some importance, always look for how those moments fit into a bigger picture. Even Neil Armstrong's celebrity moment was part of a greater headline: "The United States Wins the Race to the Moon!"

This is an important but often-overlooked point when it comes to exploring Scripture. Too often we segment Scripture into individual stand-alone moments. It's one of the unfortunate unintended consequences of snipping Scripture into chunks and slices of chapters and verses: we view Scripture like a stack of sticky notes rather than a scrolling storyboard.

Seeing Scripture with fresh eyes often requires mentally erasing all chapter and verse markers. That's when you may be able to see a narrative flow too often obstructed by the intrusive stops and starts.

THE TWO SHALL BECOME ONE

Here's a case in point. In Mark 4:35—5:21, Mark strung together two miraculous events that we typically treat separately: Jesus calmed the storm, and Jesus delivered the demoniac. But what if the insertion of a chapter five marker inaccurately signals a stop in the action? What if those two events form one narrative and together provide an indispensable lesson?

That's what I hope to explore as we look at this section with the markers removed (with fresh eyes). It's all one flowing story about one great moment. Here are the basic events: Jesus journeyed across the Sea of Galilee, faced and eliminated a violent storm, landed on the opposite shore, encountered and exorcised a demon-possessed man, and from there proceeded on with ministry. When you simply remove the markers, something intriguing springs to the surface: Were these two events merely sequential, or is there a correlation between the violent storm and the encounter with the demoniac? This calls for some textual investigation, a search for any clues to a correlation. We find at least two. "A furious squall came up, and the waves broke over the boat, so that it was nearly swamped. Jesus was in the stern, sleeping on a cushion. The disciples woke him and said to him, 'Teacher, don't you care if we drown?' He got up, rebuked the wind and said to the waves, 'Quiet! Be still!' Then the wind died down and it was completely calm" (4:37–39).

The first clue that the storm and the demoniac's restoration might be correlated is that this threatening storm seemed beyond the ordinary. Jesus traveled in the boat with seasoned fishermen. Storms were common on this body of water, bounded by mountains that funnel winds from the north. However, the disciples' level of fear in this case suggests an abnormal intensity to the storm; it made crusty seamen tremble. Mark described it as *furious*, meaning "angry." That is a common way of characterizing violent storms but perhaps more fitting than you might first think, until you consider the way Jesus responded to this storm.

Mark chose the word *rebuke*. That was an odd way for Jesus to react. After all, a storm is a natural phenomenon caused by wind doing what it does by nature. The word *rebuke* is used when there has been willful intent behind an immoral or inappropriate act. The wind did not choose to stir up a furious squall.

An unexpected furry family addition regularly reminds me what *rebuke* really means, with my wife's help. One day a cat showed up at our patio door and adopted us as her forever family. All it took was us feeding her a couple of times, and she decided we belonged to her. Clearly we were never going to get rid of her and appropriately decided to name her Sliver. More than occasionally, Sliver kills a mouse or small bird and presents it to us for—I'm guessing—admiration. That always bothers me.

Then one day I witnessed Sliver's hunting process. She didn't just kill the mouse with one swift strike of her claws or clamping of her jaws; she maimed it. Then she batted it around for a while, hurt it a little more, tossed it, and pounced on it over and over, as though she were perfecting her skills. Until finally—who knows why?—she ended the torture by tearing off the head. Is that too graphic? Then you'll understand why I began to call Sliver "You murderer!"

My vitriol has only increased as I have seen that process repeated over and over with little squirrels, birds, moles, and more mice. Every time I inform my wife, "The murderer struck again."

But my wife, who does not share my disgust, simply replies with undeserved grace, "Don't call her a murderer. She's a cat. She's just doing what cats do."

"Hey, why are you rebuking *me*? I'm not the one chewing off the squirrel's head!"

Of course, my wife's point is the one I am making here about Jesus' way of relating to the storm. A rebuke is appropriate only when there is evil intent or negligence. You don't rebuke purely natural behavior, when something has no choice in the matter. The wind had not decided to swamp the boat and drown the people.

So why did Mark use the verb *rebuke* to describe how Jesus dealt with the wind and waves? Apparently, he recognized a similarity between that event and how Jesus spoke to demons, because Mark used the same word to describe how Jesus exorcised the disruptive demon that could not contain itself when He taught in the Capernaum synagogue (Mark 1:25). Plus, He scolded the waves, "Be still!" with the same word He used to scold that demon.

This provides one piece of evidence that something else is going on during the sea-crossing moment. That "something else" becomes clearer and more convincing when Jesus and the disciples disembark on the lake's eastern shore: "They went across the lake to the region of the Gerasenes. When Jesus got out of the boat, a man with an impure spirit came from the tombs to meet him" (5:1–2).

After a detailed and shocking description of the condition of the man (often referred to as the demoniac) and his bizarre behavior (see previous chapter), Mark continued to describe his actions. Mark reported, "When he saw Jesus from a distance, he ran and fell on his knees in front of him. He shouted at the top of his voice, 'What do you want with me, Jesus, Son of the Most High God? In God's name don't torture me!'" (vv. 6–7).

The moment Jesus' toes touched damp sand, a shockwave of fear forced the stumbling demoniac out of his seaside den. The demoniac knew the Son of God was coming and who He was. How did he know? Who tipped him off?

We learn later that this poor fellow's body is the physical address of a whole "legion" of demons. A first-century Roman legion consisted of about five thousand soldiers. Think about that. This is the first time Jesus set foot in that Gerasene region, and the moment He landed, thousands of enemy demons recognized their doom, rushed out of the darkness, and pled for mercy through the voice of their helpless host. Some kind of reconnaissance communication must have been going on in a spiritual dimension even before Jesus' beach landing.

A BIG FLAK ATTACK

Now let's combine these two events that seem inappropriately separated by a chapter marker and in light of the textual evidence consider a possible unifying scenario. First, a rebuke-worthy, furious storm arose that could have thwarted Jesus' progress across the lake toward new territory. Second, a demon-infested man knew Jesus was coming, He was the Son of God, and He was about to wipe out the opposition. Does this not sound like all one event rather than two?

Near the end of World War II, the Allied forces engaged in bombing missions to destroy factories and command centers deep in the heart of Germany. We've seen the old movies where a squadron of B-17s flies in formation toward its target, and as the bombers close in, the skies fill with flashes and thunder of antiaircraft gunfire—so-called flak—intended to prevent the bombers' destructive arrival. It's all one mission: the flight toward the concentration of enemy power, the encounter with ineffective destructive flak, and the release of explosive power that wipes out enemy war-making ability.

This is exactly what we see when we don't separate the miracle of Jesus' calming the winds and the waves and the miracle of the healing of the demoniac. Jesus intentionally, almost abruptly, got in the boat on the sea's western side where all His ministry had been concentrated to cross over to new territory. He appears to be on mission. He suddenly faced the flak of malevolent winds and waves, but their fury proved ineffective. He proceeded to a very specific target where there was a concentration of demonic power, and He destroyed it. It appears to be all one event, not two.

THE INVASION PATTERN

I believe this cosmic scenario is true to the text. But it should do more than impress us with high drama, for it also instructs us. The cosmic dimension of these two miracles shows what God intends when the gospel ministry of Jesus enters new territories in the lives of people like you and me. In other words, there is a pattern to God's saving work.

Let's imagine a scenario in which a troublesome area of sin in a person's life needs to be eliminated. This "invasion" narrative presents the following four-stage, hopeful picture of what can happen.

Enemy Interference

Our souls' Enemy will not sit idly by and let us engage Christ's power, which works in us to "will and to act in order to fulfill his good purpose" (Phil. 2:13). He will stir up winds of interference of some sort when we invite God to work in new territories of character or behavior. That interference may be situational (e.g., life distractions, busyness), psychological (e.g., discouragement, doubt), intellectual (e.g., confusion, cynicism), or theological (e.g., "there is no such thing as demonic interference").

Whatever form the interference might take, it will initially toss you about. But as a follower of Jesus Christ, you can voice His authority to disempower enemy interference with simple prayers, even by just speaking Jesus' name aloud in the situation. The Holy Spirit affirms through Scripture that "at the name of Jesus every knee should bow" (v. 10), including beings who have no physical knees.

Root Causes Exposed

Just as the demoniac rushed out of the darkness into the light, no evil power or influence can remain hidden in the Son of God's presence. It must reveal and identify itself.

As a pastor, I have walked alongside many people who have suffered physical ailments that could not be diagnosed for a time. If and when the doctors finally identified the problem, great relief and hope rushed in. Why? An accurate diagnosis opens the door to effective treatment. The same is true for our struggles with spiritual ailments. When a person understands the root cause of their susceptibility to certain temptations and their struggle with discouraging sin habits, their release and relief are more likely. That's because the cause of our struggle with habitual sin often is not what we think it is.

For example, people who have an anger problem often try to get over the problem by seeking better self-control. But many people with an anger problem find that the cause is located somewhere else. But where? The good news is that the presence of the invited Spirit of Christ shines light and exposes unrecognized root causes that, once identified, can be more successfully eliminated. The Lord often works in these areas through the assistance of trained pastors and counselors, but He also gladly exposes root causes through personal prayer and fellow believers' prophetic wisdom.

Evil Powers Eliminated

The demoniac suffered greatly from evil that resided in him. Let me make that point as strongly as I can. The text clearly defines his problem as a problem with *resident* evil, not *constitutional* evil. He was a normal human being with supernormal powers of evil occupying his body. The evil was *in* him but was *not* him. Once those supernormal powers were removed, he was immediately restored to normalcy. He went from uncontrollable acts of self-mutilation and insanity to psychological peace and sanity. This wonderful fact is made powerful by how graphically his problem was described. Mark said, "No one could bind him anymore, not even with a chain. For he had often been chained hand and foot, but he tore the chains apart and broke the irons on his feet. No one was strong enough to subdue him" (Mark 5:3–4).

Most problems people have with sinful and selfish behavior can be controlled and converted into acceptable behavior by acts of the will. We can retrain, reward, remind, or remove ourselves in ways that help us do right things—even when we'd rather

not. God gave us these tools and, through His Spirit's empower-
ment, uses them in our lives. But the demoniac's problem was
different. It represents those problems that persist when normal
methods of self-control do not work. For example, many men
who struggle with pornography attempt to employ various
techniques and external controls to keep themselves from sexual
sin. But they still keep breaking those self-imposed chains. The
rule of thumb is this: when normal methods of self-control
aren't effective, you know at some level a spiritual power must
be arrested and removed from any position of influence.

The wonderful news is that these are exactly the kinds of
problems that are fixed if the power of the gospel is unleashed
in a person's life. When people do not experience the full
emancipating power of the gospel and struggle unsuccessfully
against chronic sin, they often say with resignation—a resignation prompted by what is too often the church's conventional
wisdom on the matter of chronic sin—"I am a sinner, and I will
have to deal with this problem until I die."

But that certainly contradicts what this narrative portrays.
This miracle reveals that gospel power should result in redemp-
tion not resignation. Jesus wants to bring His righteous presence
into every region of your personal geography. And when He
comes, evil must be exposed and eliminated. But there's one
more stage of this wonderful gospel. It's the one we covered in
the previous chapter. Let me remind you.

Experiential Evidence of Transformation

When Jesus brings the power of gospel ministry into a person's life, he or she is not left to guess, *Am I a changed person?* The Lord loves to provide evidence that strengthens your grip of faith on His promises and provision for ongoing freedom and transformation.

JESUS' INCREDIBLE PRIORITY

Isn't this wonderful news? And it's all right here in this one event composed of two miracles. But the news gets even better. I want to show you one more verse. It's one that does not get associated with this event, once again because of the pesky problem of somewhat arbitrary text divisions. So unfortunately, our subdivided Bibles close out the demoniac's story with verse 20 of Mark 5: "So the man went away and began to tell in the Decapolis how much Jesus had done for him. And all the people were amazed."

This sounds like a good place to stop, except the story is not actually over until we read on to verse 21: "When Jesus had again crossed over by boat to the other side of the lake, a large crowd gathered around him while he was by the lake."

Do you see it? What did Jesus do immediately after healing the demoniac and destroying the demonic stronghold? He sailed back the way He had come across the lake. Why is that significant? It tells us when Jesus originally got in the boat to go to the region of the Gerasenes to destroy that evil stronghold, that was the *only* thing He planned to do.

You would think He might have stayed to carry on some other work. But no. He journeyed across the lake, neutralized the enemy, and went back. He had one thing on His mind: to wipe out an enemy stronghold. By ignoring the chapters and verses and looking for when a story naturally begins and ends, in this case seeing Jesus' movement and timing, we gain a very clear picture of the intention behind His travel plans. We see His priorities. He was—and is—out to destroy enemy strongholds wherever they exist!

It turns out that this story provides a visual template of something the apostle John saw clearly about the Son of God's incarnation: "The reason the Son of God appeared was to destroy the devil's work" (1 John 3:8).

One day Jesus crossed a large body of water to do one thing—destroy the enemy stronghold—and then returned to where He had come from. Similarly, but much more grandly, one day Jesus crossed a large chasm between heaven and earth to do one thing—destroy the Devil's works—and then returned to where He came from.

Without a doubt, it was a grand day when Neil Armstrong stepped foot on the surface of the moon. But how much greater was that day the Son of God stepped foot on earth? He came to reclaim every inch of this oppressed planet for His kingdom. The time Jesus vanquished the storm and liberated the demoniac is just one representative moment of God's eternal travel plans.

Those travel plans still play out today for you and me. No enemy stronghold can remain when Jesus arrives, and He would love to cross into any territory in your life to set you free.

20/20 FOCUS

1. It's always encouraging to see how determined the Lord is to accomplish His purposes. Can you think of other biblical instances when God's determination was demonstrated?

2. Satan is a formidable opponent who tries to keep people from experiencing spiritual freedom and wholeness. Where might you still be facing resistance to transformation?

3. As this chapter revealed, eliminating evil power is Jesus' priority. He is ready and willing to

make a special trip to deliver even just one person or to tear down one area of bondage in a person's life. Who would you like Jesus to focus on? In what area of that person's life?

Lord, the matter-of-fact way in which You go about Your work of overpowering our Enemy astounds me. The battle is not always a long, drawn-out siege. It can be as simple as saying, "Be quiet!" I'd like You to direct Your delivering power in the direction of _____. Thank You that I don't have to beg for this. It's already Your primary mission. I will trust that You are already on the way. Amen.

VISION CHECK

"Read it like a letter," a Bible teacher once instructed our group as he handed out a version of Colossians stripped of chapter and verse numbers. He said, "When Paul wrote, he didn't include chapters and verses." Those reference points, while helpful locators, trigger the analytical part of the brain. With the dividing references removed, you can see new, previously overlooked connections between passages.

For example, mentally erase the verse and chapter numbers in Luke 10:38—11:13 and search for what theme and lessons connect those normally disconnected passages. Then compare your observations with mine on dougnewton.com or the Fresh Eyes app.

7

A CURE FOR CAN'T

Healing the Demon-Possessed Boy
Matthew 17:14–20; Mark 9:14–29; Luke 9:37–43

Want to improve your effectiveness?
There's a scary but helpful question
you absolutely must learn to ask.

All my life I've heard statements like this from churches and Christian ministries: if even one person comes to faith in Jesus Christ through our efforts, then it will all have been worth it. Maybe you have heard that too. But is it true?

If you have played chess before, you know a common strategy is to sacrifice a chess piece, like a pawn or knight or bishop, if it means winning the match. God's Enemy is more than willing to trade one person coming to faith if he can keep a hundred away from God. So he is pleased when some Christian or Christian group continues using shoddy literature, shaming tactics, or questionable financial practices just because they can point to a couple of success stories.

In God's kingdom, success can be measured *quantitatively*, or in numerical terms. I do not limit success to the number of conversions. The degree or quality of life transformation can also be measured. The apostle Paul wrote of being changed from "one degree" of glory to the next (2 Cor. 3:18 ESV). While those "degrees" can be identified *qualitatively*, or by their subjective qualities, that doesn't mean they can't be measured. A person can change from showing Christlike patience one out of five stressful times to showing patience three out of five times. A person can change from being someone who turns away moderate wrath with a soft answer to someone who gives a soft answer even when that wrath is severe. While we may not have formal assessment measures like these, we still "measure" transformation by casual observation.

Believe me, most pastors have high but often-disappointed hopes that the people of their congregations will grow in Christian character or increase the spirit of servanthood or learn to forgive at least twenty times seven, even if they can't make it all the way to seventy times seven. These things suggest the effectiveness of ministry, and they are perceived quantitatively.

Is this not what Jesus told His disciples? In the well-known chapter on fruit-bearing (John 15), Jesus said true disciples are revealed through both their quantitative and qualitative effectiveness: "This is to my Father's glory, that you *bear much fruit* [quantity], showing yourselves to be my disciples" (v. 8). "You did not choose me, but I chose you and appointed you so that you might go and bear fruit—*fruit that will last* [quality]" (v. 16).

Any Christian, church, or Christian ministry has a God-given obligation to bear as much fruit as possible. This requires a willingness to ask the question: Are we as effective as possible? Let's use this question of effectiveness versus ineffectiveness as we approach the miracle of Jesus delivering a young boy from a tormenting demonic spirit. The question should help you see this miracle with fresh eyes.

As the three Synoptic Gospels—Matthew, Mark, and Luke—report, this story spins on the axis of ineffectiveness. A young boy's father had brought his son to Jesus' disciples, begging them to exorcise a destructive demon from his son, but they failed (Matt. 17:16; Mark 9:18; Luke 9:40).

That failure led to frustration and conflict. The father was frustrated with the disciples. And so was Jesus! But notice that the disciples' failure led to conflict with the religious scholars. In fact, that's what drew an animated crowd in the first place: "When they came to the other disciples, they saw a large crowd around them and the teachers of the law arguing with them.… 'What are you arguing about with them about?' he asked" (Mark 9:14, 16).

We don't know for sure what they argued about. If the authorities were acting true to form, they might have been contending that unlearned blue-collar workers like the disciples had no ability or authority to exorcise demons in the first place: "That's why you failed."

By the way, had the disciples been successful, there would have been no conflict. Have you ever noticed conflict tends to break out in the church after a perceived failure? When the building project doesn't produce increased giving as promised, when the pastor preaches on healing and no one gets healed, or when a switch to contemporary worship doesn't bring in more young families, people start to argue. Failure creates critics.

The disciples' failure gave the religious teachers ammunition. They would have had nothing to say if the disciples had been effective. Even Jesus became a critic. "'You unbelieving and perverse generation,' Jesus replied, 'how long shall I stay with you and put up with you?'" (Luke 9:41).

All three gospels record the same words. Jesus' rebuke must have scarred their egos. "Unbelieving"? "Perverse"? Harsh! The Greek word translated *perverse* means "terribly twisted." The apostle Paul used it to admonish a sorcerer named Elymas, who tried to prevent Paul's delivery of God's Word. "You are a child of the devil and an enemy of everything that is right!" Paul said. "You are full of all kinds of deceit and trickery. Will you never stop perverting the right ways of the Lord?" (Acts 13:10).

Jesus' frustration couldn't be contained in just those two words, however. It got worse. How would you like it if someone said, "How long shall I put up with you?" Clearly He was claiming the disciples should have effectively delivered the boy from his torment.

What was the torment? Even though people have tried to equate the boy's problem with something like epilepsy, the text does not allow it. Yes, part of the description sounds similar. Harmonizing the three gospel accounts paints the following picture: "A spirit that has robbed him of speech

seizes him and he suddenly screams; it throws him into con-
vulsions so that he foams at the mouth, gnashes his teeth, and
becomes rigid. It scarcely ever leaves him and is destroying
him. He often falls into the fire or into the water" (Luke 9:39;
Mark 9:17–18; Matt. 17:15).

Based on the description alone, we might treat this as a
neurological problem. But Jesus' approach to saving the boy
does not allow for that. He directly rebuked a demonic spirit
and commanded the entity to leave the boy and not come
back. "He rebuked the impure spirit. 'You deaf and mute
spirit,' he said, 'I command you, come out of him and never
enter him again.' The spirit shrieked, convulsed him violently
and came out. The boy looked so much like a corpse that
many said, 'He's dead'" (Mark 9:25–26).

Later when the disciples asked why He was successful,
Jesus referred to the problem as a specific kind of demonic
intrusion: "He replied, '*This kind* can come out only by
prayer'" (v. 29).

Some people suggest that Jesus didn't know what we know
today about neurological and physical disorders, incorrectly
attributing them to demons. Or if He knew, He chose to
operate within His audience's worldview. However, we cannot
reinterpret the passage any other way without damaging the text
or making Jesus out to be a liar. Jesus, the bodily presence of the
all-wise, all-knowing God, spoke to a spirit. Jesus healed many
people and addressed their problems as physical. He did not see

all maladies as being caused by demons. But in this situation, He did. And if that wasn't the case, it means Jesus led people (including us) to believe something untrue.

From within our modern scientific worldview, we may be inclined to rule out or severely downplay the reality of demonic forces at work in some, if not many, cases of human suffering. But Jesus did not, and that was a big part of His effectiveness.

At this point we should address the question about having more effective ministries personally and corporately in our churches. This miracle confronts us with two lessons we often fail to learn—two requests we neglect to make—rendering us ineffective. One deals with our doubt, the other with our pride.

REQUEST ONE: HELP

In Mark's version of the exorcism, Jesus looked the father in his eyes and challenged his skepticism. "'How long has he been like this?' 'From childhood,' he answered. 'It has often thrown him into fire or water to kill him. But if you can do anything, take pity on us and help us.' "'If you can"?' said Jesus. 'Everything is possible for one who believes.' Immediately the boy's father exclaimed, 'I do believe; help me overcome my unbelief!'" (vv. 21–24).

Despite his skepticism, the father made the correct request: "Help me overcome my unbelief." This is one of two requests we must learn to humbly ask in the face of our ineffectiveness, which often traces back to some way in which we are not believing God's Word. This deliverance miracle, for example, confronts our modern rejection of, or at least skepticism about, the existence of demons. We habitually assume any human failure has natural causes that can be identified and rectified through better training, tools, or techniques. However, both Jesus' and the early church's ministries and teaching require that we take demonic interference seriously as we face human need and as we seek to perform kingdom ministry effectively. If you struggle to believe that, then the proper request is "Help my unbelief."

Besides finding the needed proof in the pages of Scripture, we can also find an unbroken chain of confirmation through the classic writings of church leaders over the centuries up to and including the present day. Early church historian Justin Martyr described ordinary Christians "rendering helpless and driving the possessing devils out of the men, though they could not be cured by all the other exorcists, and those who used incantations and drugs."[1] The early Christian apologist Tertullian wrote of Christians' power through "naming the name of Christ" to cause demons to "leave at our command the bodies they have entered."[2] Augustine of Hippo said, "These false and deceitful mediators … contrive to turn us aside and hinder our spiritual progress."[3] John Calvin warned against carelessness or faintheartedness regarding the number and untiring zeal and craftiness of demons. He wrote, "We have to wage war against an infinite number of enemies, lest, despising their fewness, we should be too remiss to give battle, or, thinking that we are sometimes afforded some respite, we should yield to idleness."[4]

Our modern-day minds are soaked in scientific rationalism, so we often doubt or avoid the number of supernatural realities found in Scripture. We are the progeny of several generations of skeptics, including biblical scholars who made it their mission to cleanse the Bible of the miraculous. However, in doing so, they gutted the very text they attempted to grasp. The supernatural elements woven throughout the Bible are like a book's binding: remove the binding and the whole book falls apart.

We must believe in the supernatural realm, including the existence of demons, not only to align with Scripture and historic Christianity but also to effectively minister. If indeed it is true as the apostle Paul said that "our struggle is not against flesh and blood" but against spiritual powers (Eph. 6:12), if indeed as the apostle Peter warned our Enemy prowls about to devour believers (1 Pet. 5:8), and if almost every advance of Jesus was met with demonic opposition, then we are doomed to failure of all sorts if we do not heed the realities of and effectively confront the spiritual powers that oppose God's will.

My first lesson in this regard occurred dramatically one Sunday night years ago as I conducted a Bible study on John 3:16. In the group sat a young mom who, to my surprise, did not understand the gospel of salvation by faith. She made a comment about working to earn God's grace that tipped me off.

I was about to respond, but another group member beat me to the punch, turned toward the young mom, and gently shared the gospel of free grace through Jesus' work on the cross. It took only a minute and then we moved on.

A year later I had a conversation with the same young mom that unexpectedly returned to that John 3:16 Sunday evening. To my shock, I discovered this young mom had been nursing a grudge against the older Christian woman who shared the gospel so lovingly that night. When I asked why, the young mom grew angry and accused the older woman of cursing at her and spitting on her in the course of her gentle witness. She also added how disappointed she was that I did not step in to stop the abuse.

Although I had no previous experience of this sort, I discerned some malevolent interference and asked the young woman a diagnostic question—"Have you ever dabbled in Ouija boards, tarot cards, or séances?" That's when I uncovered her exposure to some occult practices and was able to carefully lead her out of spiritual deception. Her life was transformed. Up until then I had no idea that enemy forces could disrupt the transmission of gospel words being sent across the airwaves. The brilliant philosopher-theologian Thomas Aquinas wrote: "Demons can effect a change in a man's imagination and even in his bodily senses, so that something appears to be other than it is."[5]

Certainly we all need more faith than we currently have in many areas. Effectiveness begins by asking the Lord to identify and deal with whatever doubts we have: "Help me overcome my unbelief." However, in particular we must shed our skepticism about satanic interference. If we refuse to recognize and properly combat the oppositional schemes of God's Enemy, we will move blindly toward ineffectiveness and discouragement.

REQUEST TWO: WHY?

The disciples brought the story's second request: "Why couldn't we drive it out?" (Matt. 17:19; Mark 9:28). By combining Matthew's and Mark's accounts, we get this mind-stretching response that immediately captures our attention: "[Jesus] replied, 'Because of your little faith. For truly, I say to you, if you have faith like a grain of mustard seed, you will say to this mountain, "Move from here to there," and it will move, and nothing will be impossible for you'" (Matt. 17:20 ESV). "This kind can come out only by prayer" (Mark 9:29).

Unfortunately, the urge to understand Jesus' meaning and how far to take it (i.e., literally throwing around mountains) pulls our attention from the profound power of the disciples' question. Their question is flat-out the most important yet most avoided question anyone who wishes to face the issue of ineffectiveness can ask. It often goes unasked, however, because it requires a great deal of courage and humility: *Why did I fail?*

Some people are only willing to ask themselves this question privately. But when they stop with that, they open the door to rationalization, self-justification, and blame-casting and miss key truths. It takes real nerve to ask someone other than yourself, "Why did I fail? What did I do wrong? How should I have done things differently?"

Among my hardest undertakings as a leader was to ask my staff to evaluate me … anonymously. Goodness knows, across the years I have always wanted my coworkers to recognize how hard I worked to be a good boss and do everything well so that they were pleased with me, my efforts, and my abilities. Anything less than a strong affirmation of those facts would have been a blow. On one occasion, that's exactly what happened. Would I ever do that again? Yes, I have to, or I might live in self-deception.

Most people, in every kind of employment, get evaluated from time to time. But I'm talking about asking for it not just accepting it when thrust on you. As shallow as their understanding and flimsy as their faith may have been, these disciples brought Jesus the perfect question in the face of their ineffectiveness: "Why were we ineffective?"

After years of pastoral counseling, I am convinced the question, "How should I do things differently?" if asked humbly would have solved most of the marital problems, emotional struggles, and psychic confusion that brought people to my office.

In the Christian life, we are supposed to accomplish a host of important tasks. Each of us has various roles to play and purposes to fulfill. When we have times of failure or experience the unpleasant signs of ineffectiveness, when we otherwise could and should be effective, posing two questions may cure the can't: "Where do I lack faith?" and "Why have I failed to be more effective?"

Try humbly asking those questions—not just to yourself but also to others—sincerely wanting to hear whatever the Lord or some other people may say, and you'll be well on your way to effectiveness. Don't miss that shortly after this miracle, Jesus sent out the larger group of seventy-two disciples and they returned thrilled to have discovered their power over demonic forces (Luke 10:17). Their success proves they must have taken Jesus' diagnosis ("This kind can come out only by prayer") to heart and learned their lesson.

20/20 FOCUS

1. Which one of the quotes about demons from earlier Christian thinkers was most interesting, shocking, or powerful to you? Why?

2. Think about a responsibility or role in which you were told you were (or were made) ineffective. Did you ever ask why? If so, what did

the person you asked say? If not, would you be willing to ask someone?

3. Of course, it's usually a cop-out to blame our failures on the Devil. However, there's no reason to let the pendulum swing to the opposite extreme and never consider satanic interference. Satan preys on our natural fears and weaknesses to make us ineffective. Is there some area where you're especially susceptible to his schemes?

Lord, I want my efforts to serve others to be fruitful. No doubt I am often like the disciples. Partly successful. Partly not. I'd like the percentages to improve. I know You're not asking for perfection, but I also know it pleases You when I achieve what You make possible. When I fall short, help me to be humble enough to ask why and listen honestly. Amen.

VISION CHECK

Often two or more gospels record the same event but tell it differently. That's when it's important to harmonize, or blend, the accounts.

Start with one of the accounts, usually the one with the most detail, as your baseline and then add words or phrases from the other gospels that don't show up in the baseline passage. Then consider why one author included a fact or comment while another didn't. In most cases a more comprehensive picture of the one event emerges, helping you view the story in 3-D.

Here's a challenging exercise. All four gospels tell the story of Jesus' baptism: Matthew 3:13–17; Mark 1:9–11; Luke 3:21–22; John 1:32–34. Put them all together. Color-code them if need be and see what they all have in common. What insights come out of those observations? Check dougnewton.com or the Fresh Eyes app to compare your insights with what I discovered.

8

FAITH IN FAITH

Healing the Woman
Mark 5:21–34

Some people warn us to put our
faith not in faith, just in God. Is
that what Jesus would say?

I pulled up behind a car with a bumper sticker that read, "Life is terrific. Business is great. People are wonderful." Apparently, the man and woman in the car had not read their bumper sticker in a while, because they spent the entire red light cycle screaming at each other. The way they were going at it—spit-sprayed invectives shooting everywhere—they needed windshield wipers inside the car. I thought, *Life is terrific, huh? People are wonderful? Hey, you two, your behavior doesn't match your bumper sticker.*

That scene is not unlike how the church appears to the world: hey, you people, your behavior doesn't match your bumper sticker. Many of us live with a haunting, taunting sense that the onlookers are right, especially when it comes to how we say our faith should work. Our bumper sticker reads, "Peace is incredible, contentment is constant, and problems are solved."

But anxiety, frustration, discontent, and unsolved problems fill our lives, and we accept this! Why? If we came home from a superstore with an appliance that didn't work, we would take it back for an exchange or refund. But for some reason ineffective faith doesn't make us wonder whether we should exchange our beliefs about faith for something better—a faith that works—and keep doing that until our bumper sticker rings true. Sadly, instead, we weaken our theology. That is to say, we change our bumper sticker to read something truer to our experience: "Peace is elusive, contentment is sporadic, and problems are overwhelming."

That's just the way it is. Get used to it.

The world needs to see something that works. People will flock to it. They need to see Christians who live with a genuine sense of God's presence, reflecting Christlike qualities and contented spirits, offering compassionate service that solves problems and changes lives.

Nothing depicts "faith that works" better than the story we are about to examine of the woman with a twelve-year hemorrhage. To see this miracle with fresh eyes, we need to prepare ourselves to view faith differently than we commonly do. While faith can be expressed through statements, faith is primarily action, not axioms.

Consider this. Christianity grew explosively in the first century before many of its core doctrines were clarified and codified. Many of the propositions we now say people need to affirm to be Christians were unknown to most people who brought their friends and neighbors to faith in Jesus as Lord and Christ. How could that be?

Scholars often say that Paul's letter to the Romans presents the most thorough expression of systematic theology found in the New Testament. How did it come to be that kind of document? Clearly the Roman church at that time did not understand what they needed to believe. Paul had to supply fundamental theological truths and straighten them out. That was important and right. Yet long before Paul's letter, without any on-site apostolic influence, the church had grown fruitfully. Their faith was evidently theologically poor yet evangelistically rich. How did that happen?

Don't get me wrong. The faith propositions the church eventually hammered out, like the Apostles' Creed, are foundational and essential for the propagation and preservation of true Christianity around the world and across the centuries. But propositions are not faith. If you think I am adamant on this point, wait until you discover what Jesus did and said during one miraculous healing: "A large crowd followed and pressed around [Jesus]. And a woman was there who had been subject to bleeding for twelve years. She had suffered a great deal under the care of many doctors and had spent all she had, yet instead of getting better she grew worse" (Mark 5:24–26).

This heart-wrenching account tells of a person in bondage, not just a person with a physical problem. For twelve years, she woke up every day to the inconvenience, embarrassment, shame, and loneliness of her physical condition. Can you imagine a life in which you couldn't even sit down without risking embarrassment? Can you imagine living with the stigma of being untouchable lest you make others ceremonially unclean?

Your own husband would have to choose between romantic affection, even a compassionate touch, and religious devotion. She had every right to cry out, "How long?" She had a reason to tear at the sky with her fingernails, clawing for divine attention, begging for relief.

When heaven above failed to respond, she did everything possible to find help below. She exhausted all her resources traveling from doctor to doctor in search of the solution to her problem. Don't think about doctors like today, however. There was no American Medical Association. No board of ethics. No standardized research. According to historians, some remedies those doctors might have suggested were

- "drinking a goblet of wine containing a powder compounded from rubber, alum and garden crocuses"

- administering a "dose of Persian onions cooked in wine … with the summons, 'Arise out of your flow of blood!'"

- creating a "sudden shock"

- "carrying … the ash of an ostrich's egg in a certain cloth"[1]

When everything ran out, from her money to her hope, the only thing left flowing was her blood. She looked not only behind at a trail of stained years but also ahead to many more of the same. That's why the narrative refers to her physical problem as bondage. She was "subject" (Mark 5:25) to the bleeding and "suffered a great deal" even "under the care of many doctors" (v. 26). So when Jesus cured her problem, Mark referred to her not as being healed but rather as being "freed" (v. 29).

She was desperate for the chains confining her to be broken, and Jesus was her last hope. She had no idea who Jesus really was or how He could possibly heal her. But she had to try anything, and this option was free. So she risked making everyone in the crowd angry with her, making Jesus angry with her, and having her hopes dashed one more time. She pressed through the crowd and reached out, assuming that even touching His robe's hem would be sufficient (v. 28). Instantly, she knew she was healed. She felt something—some power?—course through her body (v. 29).

At that moment, Jesus felt power leave His body (v. 30). Someone had plugged in to His energy source without His invitation. The woman wasn't prepared for Him to stop in His tracks and demand to know who touched Him. Even when His disciples tried to persuade Him to move on, He insisted on finding the person who touched Him. Most likely the woman assumed He was angry and intended to at least scold her, if not punish her in some way. She probably wanted to run. But pushing through the crowd, away from Jesus, would be as obvious as yelling out, "Here I am!" So she had no choice but to fall at His feet. Quaking but pouring out words, she "told him the whole truth" (v. 33), hoping to be spared from harm.

Turns out all Jesus wanted was to connect with her, to set her mind straight and her heart at ease. Given Jesus' modus operandi, this offered a great teaching opportunity for His disciples as well. The reassurance He wanted to offer and the lesson He wanted to convey concerned the power of simple, focused faith. That, according to Jesus, brought her healing (v. 34). Her desperation birthed and pointed her faith in Jesus' direction. No credit to her, though; she didn't know Jesus was the *right* direction. She lucked out. Her faith was not based on sound doctrine and believing all the right things. Plus, she did not come to Him as Lord, promising ongoing obedience. She merely wanted deliverance, and she tried Jesus.

If we take this story at face value and Jesus' comment as raw truth, then we are left with one simple way of describing faith: faith is an act of focused desperation born of utter helplessness. Faith, often with little knowledge, involves lunging for God's powerful grace. That's exactly what Jesus said: "Your faith has healed you" (v. 34).

But isn't that an oversimplification bordering on error? Certainly it wasn't *only* her faith that caused the healing. If she had lunged for any other Jew but Jesus, nothing would have happened. Why didn't Jesus clarify that? Why didn't Jesus make

sure she knew who He was? He could have said, "Please understand, woman, I am the Son of God, which is the only reason
you are healed right now."

But He didn't do that. He created a dramatic moment—
"Stop the music!"—and would not rest until He had delivered
this message: "Your faith—your idea that all you had to do was
touch My cloak, your risking everything to push through the
crowd even though you don't really know who I am and have not
actually made any commitment to follow Me—has healed you."

JUST ONE CAUSE?

Was Jesus wrong? Did He not understand the complexity of
causation—that any effect usually has more than one cause?
Aristotle did. He famously taught how any effect has four
types of causes: material, formal, efficient, and final. If Aristotle
understood the complexity of causation, certainly the Son of
God did.

Think of it this way: When you get in your car to drive
to the store, what causes your car to move toward the store?
Certainly you, the driver. If you hadn't gotten into the car, the
car would have gone nowhere.

But then what about the engine? Unless you have a car like
Fred Flintstone's, you can sit behind the wheel, shift it into
drive, and push on the gas pedal all you want, but it will go

nowhere without an engine. So is it the driver or the engine that causes the car to go?

And then there are the other components of a car. The key. No key and the engine doesn't start. Why else do we feverishly hunt for lost keys? But even if you have a key, without gas the engine won't start. Or you can have a key, gas, and an engine, but if you don't have a transmission, the car goes nowhere. So what *causes* the car to go?

And don't forget the more abstract causes. Think of all the laws of chemistry and physics, like combustion or $F = ma$. Without those, not only the car but the whole universe would be at a standstill.

Finally, think about the driver. People don't get in a car just to get in a car. They get in a car to go somewhere. They have a reason. The need to buy a gallon of milk, which causes the key to turn, the engine to start, the transmission to shift, and the car to go forward. What is the cause? All of these.

So when Jesus said to the woman, "Your faith has healed you," He certainly knew there was a string of causes. She could have wanted to get to Jesus, but if she hadn't had working feet, she couldn't have gotten there. If she hadn't had hands, she couldn't have touched His cloak. Jesus could have said, "Your feet and hands have made you well."

But then if she had not been ailing, she wouldn't have been healed, because she would have had no reason to go to Jesus. Or if she had never heard about Jesus being nearby, she would never have gone to Him. Perhaps Jesus should have said, "Your neighbor who told you I was in town has made you well."

Then of course, as I have already pointed out, if her goal had not been Jesus, she would not have been healed. And more mysteriously, yet certainly a fundamental factor, if it had not been God's will for her to be healed, she would not have been healed. Shouldn't Jesus have said, "God's will gave you the faith to reach out and has made you well"? In other words, there were many causes.

JUST ONE CAUSE BECAUSE ...

So why did Jesus isolate just one of many causes—her faith? If we factor in the many other times Jesus emphasized the importance of faith (Matt. 8:13; 9:2, 29; 15:28; Mark 10:52; Luke 7:50; 17:19), it appears He wants us to dial up our sense of partnership in performing His will. He was saying, "As far as you're concerned, I want you to think and act as if the only thing that counts is faith expressed in action."

Faith in God's person, promises, and purposes embodied and revealed in Jesus to the degree that we take action is the one element of causation we contribute to the fulfillment of His will. Jesus often scolded His disciples about their failure to play their part.

- When people worried about the basic neces-
sities of life, Jesus said, "You of little faith"
(Matt. 6:30).

- When the waves were flooding the boat and
the disciples thought they were going to die,
Jesus scolded, "You of little faith" (8:26).

- When Peter was walking on the water but got
scared and began to sink, Jesus reprimanded,
"You of little faith" (14:31).

- When the disciples didn't understand His
teaching and thought He was talking about
making sure they had bread with them, Jesus
said, "You of little faith" (16:8).

- When the disciples came up against a tough
case of demon possession and couldn't deliver
a little boy, Jesus really scolded them by not
only saying "You unbelieving and perverse
generation" but also adding, "How long shall
I put up with you?" He then topped it off

by telling them they couldn't exorcise the boy
"because you have so little faith" (17:17–20).

Certainly Jesus' commendation of her faith encouraged the
woman, but He probably wasn't saying it for her so much as for His
disciples—and us today. We need more faith in faith. Not more
faith than we have in Jesus, of course. However, we must *believe* in
the role faith plays in the realm of causation. It's our part of the process of God's will being done here on earth as it is in heaven. Our
faith is the engine by which God's will moves. Or maybe the gas,
or even just the gas pedal. Whatever it is, it is necessary. Believe it.

Faith is an action not an axiom. If faith is an act of focused
desperation born of helplessness, don't try to work it up by
increasing your knowledge. Instead, like the woman, increase
your sense of desperate need. Our Christian bumper sticker says
we're supposed to have incredible peace, constant contentment,
and solutions to problems. If that's not the case in your life, don't
be satisfied with anything less. Be as frustrated as the woman in
this miracle so you will do whatever it takes to connect with
Jesus. Chronic anxiety, discontent, and plaguing problems?
Believe "if I can just get close to Jesus …" That simple faith
works. That's what people are waiting to see.

You never know who's behind you watching.

20/20 FOCUS

1. Is it possible for a person to hold an errant doctrine and still be in a genuine relationship with God or bear fruit as a Christian disciple? What if they don't yet comprehend Jesus as God's Son?

2. Faith is a gift from God, but in what sense is "having it" still our responsibility?

3. It's a matter of conjecture, but what do you imagine the woman did after Jesus healed and commended her? Hint: How do we even know about her twelve years of suffering, all the doctors she saw, and all the money she spent?

4. Try to identify at least one thing you say you believe but are not acting on.

   Lord, I love the way You wanted to connect personally with this woman to affirm her courageous choice and teach this fundamental lesson about

faith. It must be that You want me to live this way
too. Would You please help me move from faith as
a set of axioms to faith as a life of action? Amen.

VISION CHECK

If you want a better idea of how a word or phrase should be
understood and applied, start collecting all the instances you
can find it in the Bible. Use an old-fashioned concordance if
you have one. Or just type the word in a Bible website's search
box. Note recurring ideas or circumstances around that word or
phrase and any new insights and greater clarity you gain.

Try doing that with the word *righteousness* as used in the
New Testament. Then go to Matthew 5:20, where Jesus said
our "righteousness" must surpass that of Pharisees, and see
what springs to mind. Compare your thoughts with mine on
dougnewton.com or the Fresh Eyes app.

9

PULL THE PORK

Catching a Boatload of Fish

Luke 5:1–11

Learn these two lessons and you will
please God more than you can imagine.

Somebody's been loading a lot of pork into our Declaration of Independence. "Pork" refers to line items that get quietly tucked into a congressional appropriations bill and that provide money for pet projects. Our legislators can't seem to pass new legislation without adding pork. Like the time one congressional representative got an appropriation of two hundred thousand dollars for a tattoo removal program in the Commerce, Justice, Science Appropriations Act.[1]

That's just politics. We get that. But "pork" in the Declaration of Independence? Yes. Not money for pet projects, per se. However, someone somehow slipped in some new "rights" beyond the Declaration's three "unalienable rights" of life, liberty, and the pursuit of happiness. As a result, average Joe Citizen thinks he has some other unalienable rights: the right to live a convenient, pain-free life; the right to feel good about himself; the right to have as much as the next guy; the right to receive a paycheck regardless of performance; the right to break his promises when unexpected challenges come along; the right to pursue his passion and realize his dreams. As much as we desire these things, they are human accretions, not Creator-endowed unalienable rights.

Yet Joe Citizen feels like a victim of injustice if these pork rights are not guarded and granted. Until someone exposes and pulls pork rights like these, they will continue to influence not only Joe Citizen but Joe Christian as well. We often sense injustice or feel discontent based on the world's standards rather than the Bible's. Without realizing it, we absorb what culture tells us we need and deserve for personal peace, fulfillment, or self-worth. We bring those expectations with us to church and into our relationship with God. Then when circumstances do not meet those expectations, we react as if we've been mistreated, as if some fundamental right is not being upheld.

Here are some examples of pork I often hear passed around among Christians:

- If you have a passion for something, God wants you to pursue it. After all, that's how He created you.

- If you're good at something, then that's how God will use you. After all, that's how He designed you.

- It's important to feel fulfilled, and because God loves you, He will see to it that you are.

Are you surprised I identify these expectations as pork? They seem so right. And often God does employ us in the direction of our passions and gifts, leading to a wonderful sense of fulfillment. But it's not a guarantee. If we think it's our right, then when our lives do not accord with these expectations, we feel frustrated, discouraged, confused, and even upset with God. So in a moment we'll explore the story of the miraculous catch of fish to recalibrate our expectations and pull these pork ideas from our minds in order to maintain a right relationship with God.

Before that, however, consider this. Did you realize that only people in a wealthy, leisure-based culture would hold these expectations? About two-thirds of the world's population live their lives without the luxury (or is it a liability?) of thinking about matters like self-worth and personal passions, or asking questions like, What kind of work am I designed to do? Their preoccupation is survival, not self-fulfillment.

A missionary friend exposed my cultural blindness one day when he overheard me ask an ordinary teenager in a depressed eastern European country, "What would you like to do for your career one day?" Surprised he had no ready response, I supplied some multiple-choice options to jump-start a reply. That's when the missionary stepped in and changed the subject.

Later he pulled me aside to dial up my cultural sensitivity a couple notches. He said, "Doug, you don't realize how you were asking a very American question. In the States, young people have so many opportunities. Self-determination is possible and normal. It makes sense that we can shape our future by choosing among an array of options. That is not the world our teenagers understand here. 'What do you want to be when you grow up?' is not a realistic question. You might as well be asking how he plans to go to the moon."

The idea that we have a right and God has a responsibility to help us follow our passions and to provide a purpose that fits our gifts is "pork" that needs to be pulled from our list of unalienable rights. The famous pastor-scholar John Wesley penned a wise prayer that captures this spirit of surrendering our rights:

> I am no longer my own, but thine.
> Put me to what thou wilt, rank
> me with whom thou wilt.
> Put me to doing, put me to suffering.
> Let me be employed by thee
> or laid aside for thee,
> exalted for thee or brought low by thee.
> Let me be full, let me be empty.
> Let me have all things, let me have nothing.
> Freely and heartily I yield all things
> to thy pleasure and disposal.[2]

Yes, God gives us gifts and inspires our passions, but the use of those gifts and passions is dependent on His purposes, permission, and timing. The Lord has promised to give us an abundant life, but He is not obligated to do this according to our preferred form of occupation and self-fulfillment. This sounds almost unbiblical to people in our culture, but our examination of the miraculous catch of fish can help us see things differently.

The story is straightforward. Jesus had been teaching a crowd of people while sitting in Simon Peter's boat anchored just offshore (Luke 5:2). When He finished, He told Peter to pull up the anchor, head for deep water, and cast his nets. Peter obeyed after momentary resistance. He tentatively said, "Master, we've worked hard all night and haven't caught anything" (v. 5).

When he did what Jesus said, the nets quickly filled with such a cord-busting catch of fish that he called for assistance from his partners in a second boat. The haul of fish nearly sank both boats (v. 7)! Everyone was astonished. But it is the ensuing exchange between Peter and Jesus that forces us to face a hard fact: this miracle was a case not of Jesus flexing His supernatural muscles but of Him orchestrating a character-shaping moment for Peter and a sobering lesson on surrender for all would-be disciples, including us. Jesus knew what He was doing.

WHO KNOWS BEST?

First, Jesus custom-designed a moment for Peter. When we skim the gospel narratives in an attempt to size up Peter, it seems obvious he was a very self-confident, impetuous person. He was the kind of guy who would jump out of the boat to walk on water when nobody else would. Some possible evidence suggests that his fellow disciples did not appreciate his "I'll be the first" attitude that bordered on arrogance. Interestingly, Matthew, Mark, and John all recounted Jesus' walk on the water. But Mark and John never mentioned the part about Peter walking on water. Only Matthew did. That obvious omission at least raises questions about whether Peter's ego didn't sometimes inflate to unpleasant dimensions in the other disciples' eyes. After all, he was the one who famously boasted, "Even if all fall away on account of you, I never will" (Matt. 26:33)! He was the one who also insisted that Jesus not stop with washing his feet but bathe him entirely (John 13:9). Apparently, his penchant for going overboard was not reserved for water-walking attempts.

Whether or not Peter's pride frustrated the other disciples, Jesus was undoubtedly aware of it. Jesus never leaves pride unchecked in any person's life. That's a lesson I have learned more times than I care to remember and that led me to write the following poem:

My ego is like Jonah,
Preferring Tarshish shores
Of fairer thoughts about myself
Than Nineveh affords.

And when I can't escape
The stormy thoughts of me,
My ego boldly pushes forth
And casts me in the sea.

"Well done, good man," I think
And float on hubris swells
Until conceit is swallowed whole
And spat upon the shoals.

So never can I swallow pride;
My pride will swallow me
Unless I'm overwhelmed by grace
In forced humility.

So I can't help but imagine that Jesus—who never wasted a miracle—had a specific purpose in getting into Peter's boat, telling him to cast out into deep water after unsuccessful all-night fishing and do it all again. He knew how Peter would react.

There are many ways to hear Peter's tone of voice when he replied to Jesus' command by saying, "But because you say so, I will let down the nets" (Luke 5:5). Given Peter's track record of prideful self-confidence, my guess is that Peter sounded less like an obedient child and more like a coworker whose tone of voice says, "I know you're wrong, but I'll do you a favor this time and do what you want."

Why do I suspect that was his attitude? Because of his reaction to the big catch of fish. Why would a person fall to his knees, overwhelmed by shame at that moment? Shouldn't it have been a moment of amazement and celebration? "Wow! This is fantastic. Thank You, Jesus!" Even if he still fell at Jesus' feet, it would have been in gratitude and joy. But for Peter to say "Go away from me, Lord; I am a sinful man" (v. 8) suggests that he was convicted about his bad attitude: *I am such a jerk. I thought Jesus didn't know what He was talking about. When am I going to learn? I actually think I know more than Jesus!*

This illustrates a kind of pork in our cultural mind-set that feeds a similar self-reliant arrogance. We believe we have a legitimate right to trust our own judgment and expertise without seeking the Lord's guidance in everything and deferring always to His superior knowledge and will. The apostle James addressed this independent spirit with one of the Bible's most specific descriptions of sin.

Now listen, you who say, "Today or tomorrow
we will go to this or that city, spend a year
there, carry on business and make money."
Why, you do not even know what will happen tomorrow. What is your life? You are a
mist that appears for a little while and then
vanishes. Instead, you ought to say, "If it is the
Lord's will, we will live and do this or that." As
it is, you boast in your arrogant schemes. All
such boasting is evil. If anyone, then, knows
the good they ought to do and doesn't do it, it
is sin for them. (James 4:13–17)

It's not that we explicitly claim to know better than or at
least as much as Jesus. That attitude is simply implicit in the
fact that we make so many decisions and plans without ever
consulting Him.

Since we believe Jesus always knew what He was doing,
most likely at least one purpose of this miracle was to over-
whelm Peter with "forced humility." The sooner we understand
that humility is one of Jesus' goals for our lives, the better. The
healthiest attitude we can adopt is that of Eli, who, expecting
punishment, still said, "He is the LORD; let him do what is good
in his eyes" (1 Sam. 3:18).

CRAFTING A CRISIS

Let's not stop there. There's more pork to be pulled from our inflated bill of rights. Jesus seemed to have another purpose to this orchestrated miracle. This time, rather than imagining the attitude behind Peter's words, let's picture this moment exactly as described. It's a simple scene. Peter stood knee-deep in the biggest boatload of fish he'd ever caught. And right then, while he was still surrounded by the most success he'd ever had, Jesus called Peter to follow Him. Jesus said, "Don't be afraid; from now on you will fish for people" (Luke 5:10).

Why is that significant? Keep in mind that before this miraculous catch of fish, the disciples had a terribly unsuccessful night of fishing. That is not the time to ask someone to change careers. Most people would probably be ready to jump ship in a New York minute under those conditions. Jesus would not ask Peter to follow Him on the heels of a terribly frustrating night of fishing. Instead, He created a situation where Peter and the others had to make a radical choice. He gave them the best catch of fish in their entire careers! Two boats nearly sank, they were so loaded down!

It's like being an architect and landing the most challenging and creative project of your career. It's like working for years as a nurse and getting promoted to head nurse. Or like being a writer whose novel every publisher has rejected, when suddenly your book is accepted and becomes a bestseller. And the next day Jesus steps up to you and says, "Now leave all this and follow Me."

Jesus! What are You doing? It's almost cruel. You gave these fishermen a taste of everything they'd ever hoped for out of their fishing careers, and then You said to leave it! But that's what He had to do. Jesus forces us to make a radical break with our plans and purposes, dreams and desires.

We are tempted to prefer a relationship with Jesus in which He follows us around our world, blessing us and our pursuits. Imagine if Simon had been a fishing entrepreneur. "Wow! What a catch!" he'd say. "Just think how Jesus could bless our lives! All we need to do is stay close to Him and then ask Him to follow us out to the seashore once a day and give hand signals directing us to just the right spot to toss in our nets! We could make a mint, and of course we'd tithe."

Yes, the Lord wants to bless us. But the cultural pork in our Christian beliefs is that it's God's responsibility to bless us with a sense of fulfillment. Ergo, having a sincere passion for some good purpose signals that we have found God's will. God wouldn't give me this burning passion if He didn't want me to pursue it, would He? Of course not, we are told. But that's pork.

The Bible presents a different principle concerning God's will. God's call comes not through a burning passion so much as through a burning bush. Just because you have a burning passion doesn't mean *you* are supposed to satisfy it. That is up to God. Most times He will; sometimes He won't. You may have to live with unfulfilled passions, even noble and selfless ones.

This lesson is built into the very fabric of the maturation process. Young adolescents face it head-on. They have burning passions they must not act on until they can do so in God's time and in His way. Passions do not, in and of themselves, define God's purposes. Plus, God's role is not to fulfill our passions, even the ones He created within us. Disciples are people who surrender all their passions for one fundamental mission: to fulfill *God's* passion.

That's how the kingdom works. The only rights we fight for are God's. We must be willing to walk away from our every hope and dream in order to accomplish His every hope and dream. So Jesus gave these fishermen an incredibly satisfying experience and created a crisis moment in which they had to make a life decision. With their minds knee-deep in what they were trying to get out of life, they had to want Jesus even more. What radical abandonment! They walked away not from empty boats but from full ones. They left everything. We too are called to leave everything behind to follow Him. Even our passions and dreams … and pork.

20/20 FOCUS

1. Give a few examples of how people become frustrated when they assume they have a "right" that's being neglected.

2. Peter's right was a boatload of fish, or material success in his career. If Jesus were to give you a "boatload" of some kind of success you've worked for and then tell you to walk away from it to follow Him, what might that be?

3. Scripture details other times God created "crisis" moments to call people to total surrender. Can you name a couple? Can you identify a crisis moment in which you were called to total surrender?

Lord, I sing songs in church about loving You more, needing You more, or wanting You more than anything else. Even as I sing them, I know they aren't completely true about me. But I want them to be. I trust You are moving me in that direction. Just help me make the right choice—the total-surrender choice—in those crisis moments and every moment in between. Amen.

VISION CHECK

In this chapter we employed several Fresh Eyes techniques from previous chapters, but none of that matters if you can't forget how you've always thought about a story. Always start by identifying what you already think; then set it aside. It's not necessarily wrong; it's just in the way.

Try this. Go to the famous verse, "Perfect love casteth out fear" (1 John 4:18 KJV) and summarize how you often hear it used. Then set that aside and go back to the whole chapter. See whether we've been applying it improperly. Check out dougnewton.com or the Fresh Eyes app to see how that compares with my observations.

10

WHY JESUS WEPT

Raising Lazarus from the Dead

John 11:1–44

God can do anything. But that doesn't
mean it's always easy on Him.

What happens to the moral strength of people who are immersed in a technology-driven culture that prizes and provides user-friendly, instantaneous access to user-focused products and experiences? When remote controls can adjust the conditions in our lives at the push of a button, we develop an aversion to hard work. When drive-up windows and online ordering allow us to acquire things we want quickly, we develop an aversion to waiting. When we can create our own playlists or online radio stations so we can listen only to the music we want to hear, when all the people in our households can watch or record whatever shows they're interested in, we don't have to be adaptable or deferential. When airbags—literal or metaphorical—surround us to minimize the effects of accidents or negligence, we don't have to face painful consequences. And speaking of pain, when a pill or an ointment exists for almost any ache or discomfort, we become conditioned to avoid pain and characterize it as an unfair intrusion.

I once spoke with a ninety-seven-year-old church member who had just had eye surgery the day before. She was quite a lady, all four feet, eleven inches of her. When she was a young girl, her family migrated from Texas to Kentucky in covered wagons to be sharecroppers. Hunger, blisters, and tattered clothes defined her growing-up years. I asked her, "Miss Flora, have you had any pain since the surgery?"

She smiled almost as if I had asked a silly question. "No," she replied. "No pain. It hurts quite a bit, but no pain." At that moment I realized we came from different planets. In her world, physical discomfort ("hurts quite a bit") didn't even qualify as pain.

I don't want to be one of those curmudgeons who go on and on about what's gone wrong with the world. But let's acknowledge this: when we live in a world where so much comes so easily, we tend to become morally weaker people—people who find it hard to choose to do what's right when it requires long waiting or difficulties.

Just as physical muscles grow weak with lack of use, so do moral muscles. Think of a barbell. If a few generations ago people could lift a hundred pounds of waiting, today we can hardly bear ten pounds of it. The problem is character and faith development for Christians requires struggle and patience. But we find these hardships intolerable in a comfort-oriented culture.

This comes as no surprise to the Lord. He understands our weakness and is not stymied by a culture that fails to shape character. No matter the times or seasons of history and cultures, He has one character development tool He always uses effectively: desperation.

Desperation moves people to do what their moral strength can't. As I look back over my life, I am convinced that no significant change, no substantive improvement, no shedding of sin would have occurred apart from desperate moments. Our Lord knows how to bring all of us to that point for our good. "Remember how the LORD your God led you all the way in the wilderness these forty years.… *He humbled you, causing you to hunger* and then feeding you with manna … to teach you that man does not live on bread alone but on every word that comes from the mouth of the LORD" (Deut. 8:2–3).

"God causes us to hunger and then feeds us" should be an axiom of our faith. To people going through times of hungering, it may not seem very loving. But God's plan is to make us desperate for Him and everything that really matters, to move us when we lack moral power. With this in mind, let's turn to Jesus' miracle of raising Lazarus from the dead.

This miracle is famous not only for being the most astounding miracle of Jesus' public ministry but also for containing the Bible's shortest verse: "Jesus wept" (John 11:35). Our "fresh eyes" task is to try to understand what made Jesus cry.

WHO KNEW WHAT WHEN?

The Jews who observed Jesus' tears drew this conclusion: "See how he loved him!" (v. 36). They assumed He was grieving over Lazarus's death. Of course, that was a natural assumption, because people weeping over the loss of Lazarus surrounded the tomb. Many scholars believe Jesus felt deeply troubled and angry at death itself, even though He knew He was about to undo the death of Lazarus. Perhaps. But I think we should consider another possibility. It requires tracking back through the narrative and charting the main characters involved, where they were located, and what they knew as the events unfolded. "Now a man named Lazarus was sick. He was from Bethany, the village of Mary and her sister Martha. (This Mary, whose brother Lazarus now lay sick, was the same one who poured perfume on the Lord and wiped his feet with her hair.) So the sisters sent word to Jesus, 'Lord, the one you love is sick'" (vv. 1–3).

These three verses introduce four main characters: Lazarus, Mary, Martha, and Jesus. (Of course, there are the messengers, but they are not identified and play no significant role in the narrative, except to deliver the message.) Where were the main characters located? Lazarus, Mary, and Martha were in the village of Bethany. Where was Jesus? We can't be entirely sure of the location, but He was apparently some distance from Bethany. Most scholars assume He was about a day's walk away.

Scripture then brings a few more people into the story: "When he heard this, Jesus said, 'This sickness will not end in death. No, it is for God's glory so that God's Son may be glorified through it.' Now Jesus loved Martha and her sister and Lazarus. So when he heard that Lazarus was sick, he stayed where he was two more days, and then he said to his disciples, 'Let us go back to Judea'" (vv. 4–7).

Who are the new characters? The disciples. And where were they? They were with Jesus. We now have all the characters identified. Let's create a simple diagram and group the characters together according to where they were located.

| Jesus and the Disciples | Lazarus, Martha, and Mary |

The thick black line represents the significant geographical separation between the two groups. Now let's fill in the diagram with what these people "knew" as the events unfolded.

> So the sisters sent word to Jesus, "Lord, the *one you love is sick*."
>
> When he heard this, Jesus said, "This *sickness will not end in death*. No, it is for God's glory *so that God's Son may be glorified through it*." Now Jesus loved Martha and her sister and Lazarus. So when he heard that Lazarus was sick, *he stayed where he was two more days....*
> "But Rabbi," they said, "*a short while ago the Jews there tried to stone you, and yet you are going back?*"

Jesus answered, "Are there not twelve hours of daylight? Anyone who walks in the daytime will not stumble, for they see by this world's light. It is when a person walks at night that they stumble, for they have no light."

After he had said this, he went on to tell them, "Our friend *Lazarus has fallen asleep*; but I am *going there to wake him up.*"

His disciples replied, "Lord, if he sleeps, he will get better." Jesus had been speaking of his death, but his disciples thought he meant natural sleep.

So then he told them plainly, "*Lazarus is dead*, and for your sake *I am glad I was not there*, so that *you may believe*. But let us go to him."

Then Thomas (also known as Didymus) said to the rest of the disciples, "Let us also go, that we may die with him." (vv. 3–16)

The passage indicates the disciples knew at least nine things, listed in the left column of the following diagram. In the right column, I list eleven things Martha and Mary knew, eight of which perhaps Lazarus knew, if he was conscious during the worsening stages of his sickness. Some of these things are not explicitly stated in the text but can be assumed based on the timing of events and the reaction of the sisters when Jesus finally arrived.

What the Principal Characters Knew

Jesus and the Disciples	Lazarus, Martha, and Mary
• Lazarus was very sick.	• Lazarus was frighteningly sick.
• The sickness would not end in death.	• Jesus loved Lazarus.
• Jesus would be glorified in it.	• They had sent a message to Jesus, assuming He would come help.
• He stayed put for two days.	• If He got there in time, Jesus would save Lazarus (vv. 21, 32).
• Jesus would be heading into trouble by going near Jerusalem.	• They were waiting.
• The disciples were worried for Him.	• Jesus had not come.
• After initially misunderstanding what Jesus meant by "asleep," the disciples finally understood when Jesus told them plainly that Lazarus was dead.	• Waiting …
	• Jesus had not come.
	• Lazarus was dead.
	• Dead people stay dead.
• Jesus was glad about that.	• They were grieved and disappointed over Jesus' apparent unresponsiveness.
• Something would happen to aid their faith.	

A great value of making a chart is how it helps you condense the observations into a helpful summary. In this case, the summary statements below create a powerful contrast.

What the Principal Characters Knew

Jesus and the disciples knew everything would turn out for the good in a glorious way.	Lazarus, Martha, and Mary knew only that they had sent a request to Jesus and things had not turned out for the good because Jesus had not come in time.

This summary diagram sparked an interesting realization about what might have moved Jesus to tears. Right away I realized that the thick black line represented not only a geographical barrier but also a "knowledge of God's will" barrier. Lazarus, Martha, and Mary could not see over that barrier. Jesus had a plan to raise Lazarus, reveal His own glory, and build their faith. But Lazarus, Mary, and Martha did not know that.

And I thought, *That's just the way it is when we pray.* We send our request up over the knowledge barrier that stands between some desperate situation we face and God's undisclosed plan. We can't see over that barrier, so we usually remain in the dark as we wait for God to show up somehow. We have to believe something is going on, that God is working all things out for the good of those who love Him (Rom. 8:28), but we rarely know what or when or how.

Something important happened in my life at that moment. I found myself bowing in my heart, surrendering to "the way it's often going to be." This story is not just a New Testament episode to be enjoyed. It's a revelation of how God works most of the time, and that struck me as wonderfully okay.

I thought, *I really am okay with this.* I can be in the position of Lazarus, Martha, and Mary anytime over anything for the rest of my life, and I will be content knowing that on the other side, where my prayers can go but I can't, I have a God who loves me and is working to show His glory and build my confidence in Him.

IT HURTS TO BE LORD

That was an interesting and life-settling thought, but it also led me to see with fresh eyes what may have been behind the tears in Jesus' eyes. Stop and think:

- Jesus told His disciples that Lazarus's sickness
  would not end in death, but He did not tell
  the ones who needed to hear most. He kept
  them in the dark; they knew only that He

hadn't come and He hadn't replied. Don't you think Jesus knew what He was putting them through?

• Jesus let Lazarus die. Jesus' friends were waiting and waiting. Watching helplessly as their brother suffered and grimaced, then turned lifelessly gray. Don't you think Jesus knew what He was putting them through?

• When Jesus finally arrived, both sisters separately said to Him what they had undoubtedly spoken numerous times as they waited helplessly: "Lord, if you had been here …" Their sense of having been neglected by Jesus likely doubled their grief over their brother's death. Their words have almost the same tone as the day the waves washed over the disciples, sinking boat and they screamed, "Teacher, don't you care if we drown?" (Mark 4:38). Don't you think Jesus knew what He was putting them through?

Yes, He knew. So when He finally arrived and faced their grief and saw the disappointment in their tear-streaked faces, that's when Jesus wept. The text specifically says it was that sight that caused Him to be "deeply moved in spirit and troubled" (v. 33), not necessarily the fact of Lazarus's death but the degree of desperation He had chosen for Mary and Martha.

Of course, this is conjecture, as it always is when it comes to explaining emotions. But this hypothesis fits with what the Bible reveals about the Lord over and over again. Compassion for all of us weak and lost and helpless children fills His heart. He must do certain things to teach, train, discipline, and strengthen us in faith and character. The things He must do often leave us wondering, worrying, and waiting in desperation. It's necessary. And it hurts not just us but Him … probably even more.

RETROSPECTIVE

As I look back on my life, I am certain God has superintended all that has happened to me—the directing of my path toward the fully good goals God chose—with the divine and judicious employment of desperation. This is how it always works. We move toward God by spurts and surges sparked at points of desperation brought on directly by Him, by His gracious sculpting of our circumstances, or by the magnificently intelligent use of our best and worst choices.

This is God's way of helping us choose His will without crushing our own. Through desperation He nudges our will to the very brink of making right choices but then steps back and leaves us right there so we can participate in the thrilling leap toward the right and good and eternal. "I am the resurrection and the life.... Do you believe this?" He asked Martha (John 11:25–26).

He does not pad our falls but lets us be broken. He does not rescue us until we feel helpless. He does not shine light in the daytime but lets the darkness settle in until we cry for illumination. It seems almost cruel to our modern ears that have been trained to believe parenting is all about protecting children from all pain. But letting children cry sometimes may be the most loving act of all. And God always knows when and why and how long to let us cry.

If we are to experience the fullness of life God makes available through the Holy Spirit, we must be desperate for it. There's no use in God offering a feast for which we have no appetite. But we can't make ourselves hungry on our own. Even this comes from God. He causes and allows our hunger to grow, our thirst to deepen, and our drives to intensify and remain unfulfilled until we reach a desperate point where only one right choice will feed our starving souls. God superintends our spiritual development through the ministry of desperation. Again I say, "He humbles us, causing us to hunger, then feeds us with manna" (Deut. 8:2).

But the insight we gain from the miracle of Lazarus's resurrection is that the Lord Jesus' own sorrow ignites when He takes us deep into desperation. What love! I believe that was what was going on inside Jesus at the edge of Lazarus's tomb and resurrection. He wept for how He made them weep. And that helps me love Him even more.

20/20 FOCUS

1. This chapter suggests that the geographical distance between Jesus and Mary and Martha and their lack of understanding about what was going on symbolize what is often our experience in prayer. How often do you think this happens? Is it that way 90 percent of the time? Sixty? Forty? Is that always by God's choice?

2. Is there ever value in *not* knowing what God has in process while He's answering our prayers?

3. It is immensely difficult for people in our instant-gratification world to wait patiently. What other habits of Christian maturity are made difficult by the habits and expectations our modern culture creates?

4. Perhaps your parents said to you, "This is going to hurt me more than it hurts you." Did that mean anything to you then? I mentioned it helps me to know that Jesus weeps when He has to let us hurt. Does that help you? Why or why not?

Lord, I have to admit, I would always like to know what's going on. It's very hard to believe You're working everything out for good when I can't see You working at all. But I know that's when I have to trust Your words in Scripture. So help me keep declaring in the darkness, "You will never leave me nor forsake me. You are the light of my life. Peace that passes understanding will guard my mind in Christ Jesus." Then help me wait patiently for You, Lord. I offer my waiting as an act of worship. Amen.

VISION CHECK

It's a paradox. Creativity flows out of grunt work and rigorous effort. Jazz musicians practice before they improvise. As this chapter suggests, to get fresh insights into Scripture, you

sometimes need to do grunt work like making charts to organize observations and textual data.

Your final challenge in this book is, appropriately, a tougher
one. Read through Acts 13–21 to chart Paul's missionary trav-
els. Simply list the destinations and what made him choose
each one. After you've filled in the chart, make your observations and see whether you can draw any conclusions and learn
any lessons from Paul's decision-making process. Then hop
on dougnewton.com or the Fresh Eyes app to compare your
discoveries with mine.

NOTES

CHAPTER 1

1. Joseph Scriven, "What a Friend We Have in Jesus," 1855, public domain.

CHAPTER 2

1. T. S. Eliot, "The Hollow Men," in *The Poems of T. S. Eliot*, eds. Christopher Ricks and Jim McCue, vol. 1, *Collected and Uncollected Poems* (London: Faber & Faber, 2015), 83–84.

CHAPTER 3

1. Henry David Thoreau, *Walden* (Boston: Houghton, Mifflin and Company, 1897), 143.

CHAPTER 7

1. Justin Martyr, *The Second Apology of Justin, in The Ante-Nicene Fathers: Translations of the Writings of the Fathers down to A.D. 325*, eds. Alexander Roberts and James Donaldson, vol. 1, *The Apostolic Fathers with Justin Martyr and Irenaeus* (New York: Charles Scribner's Sons, 1903), 190.

2. Tertullian, *Apology*, trans. S. Thelwall, in T*he Ante-Nicene Fathers: Translations of the Writings of the Fathers down to A.D. 325*, eds. Alexander Roberts and James Donaldson, vol. 3, *Latin Christianity: Its Founder, Tertullian* (New York: Charles Scribner's Sons, 1905), 38.

3. Augustine, *The City of God*, trans. Marcus Dods, in *A Select Library of the Nicene and Post-Nicene Fathers of the Christian Church*, ed. Philiip Schaff, vol. 2, *St. Augustin's City of God and Christian Doctrine* (New York: Charles Scribner's Sons, 1907), 176.

4. John Calvin, *Institutes of the Christian Religion*, ed. John T. McNeill, trans. Ford Lewis Battles (Louisville: Westminster John Knox Press, 2006), I.14.14.

5. Thomas Aquinas, *Summa Theologiae*, trans. M. J. Charlesworth, vol. 15, *The World Order* (Cambridge: Cambridge University Press, 2006), 1a. 114, 5.

CHAPTER 8

1. William L. Lane, *The Gospel According to Mark: The English Text with Introduction, Exposition, and Notes*, The New International Commentary on the New Testament (Grand Rapids, MI: Eerdmans, 1974), 192.

CHAPTER 9

1. "Congressional Pig Book 2009," Citizens against Government Waste, accessed January 28, 2018, www.cagw.org/Content/Pig-Book-2009 #II_COMMERCE_JUSTICE_SCIENCE.

2. John Wesley, "A Covenant Prayer in the Wesleyan Tradition," in *Historical Dictionary of Methodism*, eds. Charles Yrigoyen Jr. and Susan E. Warrick, 2nd ed. (Lanham, MD: Scarecrow, 2005), 245.

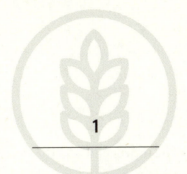

1

"HELLO, TURKEY"

The Hidden Treasure

Matthew 13:44

How can one little Bible verse capture
the full meaning of salvation?

I grew up well before the era of iPads. The closest thing we had to an attention-grabbing flat-screen instrument was an Etch A Sketch. Remember? You drew on it by turning two knobs that moved an interior stylus against the backside of a gray screen, leaving a black line. If you got good at it, you could draw almost anything, and then you simply erased the screen and started over by turning it upside down and shaking it vigorously.

This is similar to what we often must do with our minds in order to see something new or even better in a familiar Scripture passage. Case in point: "The kingdom of heaven is like treasure hidden in a field. When a man found it, he hid it again, and then in his joy went and sold all he had and bought that field" (Matt. 13:44).

One common interpretation has been "Etch A Sketched" into our minds by preachers dialing in this point: the kingdom of heaven is such a precious treasure that we, like the man, should give up everything to lay hold of it. Of course, that's absolutely true—but probably not what Jesus was talking about. So let's flip our minds upside down, shake out the old teaching, and ask the Holy Spirit to help us discover something new. Let's start with a quick review of the facts:

- *What did the man buy?* Don't say "treasure." He wanted the treasure, but he had to buy the field where he found it in order to possess the treasure. That's an important observation.

- *How did the man come up with the money to buy the field?* He sold everything he owned.

- *What was his frame of mind while doing that?* He was joyful.

- *Finally, what was the kingdom of heaven like?* Wait … don't say "treasure." The first thing you must do whenever you approach a parable that begins "the kingdom of heaven (or God) is like …" is to put the parable's elements inside a parenthesis so the phrase "kingdom of heaven" applies to everything that follows. This parable is not saying the kingdom of God is like any *one* element in the parable, such as the treasure or the man or the field. Rather, the parable is saying the whole picture that follows is what the kingdom of God is like. That is, the man finds treasure, hides it, joyfully sells everything, and buys the field. Given that basic rule of interpretation, we cannot interpret this parable the common way—that the kingdom of God should be like a treasure to us.

You might then be tempted to ask, "So what is this parable telling us to value so highly that we would give up everything to obtain it?" Here's the bad news. If you ask the question that way, you'll never arrive at the answer, because too often we don't notice any unwarranted assumptions we make. Let me demonstrate by telling you a story.

For more than thirty years, I have asked groups to solve the following "twenty-questions mystery": Mary lies dead on the floor. Tom is asleep on the couch. A colorless, odorless liquid surrounds Mary's body, and broken pieces of glass are also scattered around her. The windows and doors are all locked from the inside. What happened?

The groups always start out with the same kinds of questions. Someone asks, "Has Mary been dead a long time?"

"No, but that's not relevant to the solution," I reply.

Another person asks, "The windows may be locked, but are any of them broken?"

"Clever question. But no, none of them are broken."

"Is the liquid water?"

"Yes."

"Did Mary drop the glass before she died, because she got frightened?"

"No," I say. "But you're making an unwarranted assumption."

Eyes squint and brows furrow. Questions fly: "Is it really a house?" "Is Tom really asleep?"

"Yes," I say, "but go beyond the facts you were presented with. Who are you assuming Mary is?"

A nurse? A murderer? A thief? Eventually someone hits on it: "Is Mary a woman?"

"No." I see the light turn on.

"A little girl?"

"No."

"Is Mary human?"

"No." And there it is.

From this point, the solution comes quickly: Tom is a cat. Mary is a goldfish. Tom knocked the fishbowl off the table, it broke, and Mary died.

In the same way, our unwarranted assumption about "the man" in this parable keeps us from understanding what Jesus was teaching about God's kingdom. Here's your hint: Who are you assuming the main character to be? What if the man who bought the field is not an ordinary human being like us but the Son of God?

CHRISTUS VICTOR

What if this isn't a parable about all we must do to possess the kingdom? What if Jesus is the one who finds the treasure? What if we human beings are the treasure? What if the field is this world that belonged to Satan, the former prince of the world? And what if it is Jesus who gives up everything He owns to purchase (redeem) this world and reclaim us as His possession? What if that's what the kingdom of heaven is like?

Did you realize that for the first thousand years of Christendom that picture was likely the more common way of understanding salvation? It is sometimes called *Christus Victor*. Today the common view is *penal substitution*: that is, Jesus died in our place to pay for our sins. This view of salvation has its roots in a classic atonement theory Saint Anselm articulated in the eleventh century. After various revisions following the Protestant Reformation, it has become the dominant view of salvation. It's not that Christus Victor is right and penal substitution is wrong. They simply represent different ways of looking at the gospel. God's work of salvation is so great (Heb. 2:3), like a huge mountain, that we must view it from many angles to gain an accurate and comprehensive picture. But most Christians don't realize this and believe there is only one way to describe what Jesus accomplished on the cross.

You could summarize the Christus Victor view of salvation this way: the prince of the world, Satan, possessed this world; the Son of God came to earth and defeated him on the cross, then established and commissioned the church to enforce His kingdom's rule on earth and reclaim lost people to His possession. That used to be a more common way to understand the gospel of salvation.

When I first viewed this parable from that angle, my whole idea of salvation expanded. However, I sensed the change was so big, it was important to check my new insight against Scripture. When I did, this short parable seemed to condense several verses about Jesus' death found in Hebrews and Paul's letters:

1. ... *then in his joy went*—"For the joy set before him he endured the cross ..." (Heb. 12:2).

2. ... *and sold all he had*—"[He] did not consider equality with God something to be used to his own advantage; rather, he made himself nothing ..." (Phil. 2:6–7).

3. ... *and bought that field*—"You are not your own; you were bought at a price" (1 Cor. 6:19–20).

So my new insight checked out. As a result, I now believe penal substitution is one way to understand the gospel, but

Christus Victor is also, and it may be the most glorious understanding we have. The King of the universe reclaimed this fallen world. Isn't that exactly what Handel wrote in his celebrated "Hallelujah Chorus"?

> The kingdom of this world
> Is become the kingdom of our Lord
> And of His Christ, and of His Christ;
> and He shall reign for ever and ever.[1]

Plus, rethinking my assumptions about this parable not only resized my view of salvation but also upsized my longing to join the Lord in His treasure-seeking work. For this parable reveals our Lord's passion to reclaim us—you and me—as treasures that belong to Him. It tells of the lengths to which He will go to make a person—any person—His.

HOW FAR JESUS GOES

A couple years ago after church, a somewhat-unkempt and heavily tattooed young mom came up to me and my wife after having waited for people to clear out. Unfamiliar with church lingo and protocol, she asked cautiously, "You know your talk today?" (She didn't call it a sermon.) "Why did you look toward me and say 'Hello, Turkey'?"

I had no clue what she was talking about. I felt sure I never said such a thing. My wife's quizzical look confirmed my doubts. I just replied, "I don't remember saying that. Why do you ask?" That triggered a somewhat-lengthy description of her troubled life but how, through her ups and downs with drugs and lovers leaving her with children, she had a loving grandmother.

She went on to explain, "Gramma was someone who went to church a lot, and she prayed a lot, and I knew she loved me, but I was messed up. Last year my gramma died, but I got to see her before, and I said, 'Gramma, if I ever get back on the right track and you can see me from heaven making good choices, will you somehow tell me "Hello, Turkey"?' That's what she always used to call me. Well, this is my second week coming here to church, and this morning I clearly heard you say 'Hello, Turkey.' So I'm thinking I must be on the right track."

Her story struck me, and I told her how much God loved her and said, "Jesus knew what you asked your grandma to say. So He caused you to hear words this morning that I didn't say."

She was dumbfounded. And I was able to introduce her to this Jesus who does remarkable, miraculous things to seek and save the lost—to claim the buried treasures of this world. That's who Jesus is. That's what this parable is about. Our Lord looks at each of us as a treasure, and He will stop at nothing—pay whatever price is necessary—to help you become His possession!

Here's my suggestion: the next time you take Communion, don't think just about how much Jesus paid. Yes, it was His life He gave—it was His body that was broken and His blood that was shed. But consider *why* He paid that price. He wants you to be His. He wants you to no longer be in any kind of bondage to any form of the Enemy's power. Satan has no hold on you. He has no claim on you.

Turns out you are an Etch A Sketch yourself. When you become His, Jesus wonderfully and lovingly turns your life upside down and erases the sin, shame, corruption, and marks the Devil left in your life, granting you a clean slate and heart that He writes on by His Spirit. Because you belong to Him.

20/20 FOCUS

1. This chapter points out that the common interpretation of this parable emphasizes the enormous price a human being must be willing to pay to possess the treasured kingdom of heaven. What difference does it make to see yourself as the treasure Jesus paid to possess, rather than the kingdom being the treasure you must pay to possess?

2. The phrase "and sold all he had" was connected with Philippians 2:6–7, which speaks of the price the Son of God paid to redeem the

world. Can you think of any other Bible verses that speak of His great personal sacrifice?

3. How might things be different in our churches and among Christian believers if the Christus Victor view of salvation was more widely proclaimed and embraced in our time?

4. Take a few moments to pray for a person you would ask Jesus to seek out and save in the miraculous way He claimed the young mom in the "Hello, Turkey" story.

Lord Jesus, I am so thankful You paid the price to reclaim this world … and me. I embrace by faith my freedom from sin and from Satan's hold on me. Help me walk out that freedom in practical ways that show the world I belong to You. Amen.

VISION CHECK

Whenever you begin to think about anything, you start with assumptions you're not even aware of. The key to clear thinking is to release those assumptions. Don't let them control what you see before you check them out like we did in this parable. (Are we right to assume the man who bought the field is a person like ourselves?)

Practice this skill by going to 2 Corinthians 9:15, where Paul wrote, "Thanks be to God for his indescribable gift!" First, identify what most people assume Paul meant by the "indescribable gift" and hold it in question. Then read the preceding verses (vv. 6–14) to see if the common assumption fits the context. Or is the "indescribable gift" referring to something else? Hop on dougnewton.com or the Fresh Eyes app to compare your thoughts with mine.

NOTES

1. "C. H. Dodd," Goodreads.com, accessed February 5, 2018, www.goodreads .com/quotes/798780-at-its-simplest-the-parable-is-a-metaphor-or-simile.

2. Ireaneus quote, citation still needed (p. 10)

3. "Hallelujah Chorus," Lyrics.com, accessed February 5, 2018, www.lyrics .com/lyric/324457.

FRESH
EYES

VISIT
WWW.DOUGNEWTON.COM

- Learn more and connect with the author
- Be the first to learn about new projects
- Find out if Doug is speaking near you
- Get brand new, fresh content